AA
GLOVEBO
SPAI
POR

C000243702

contents

Map pages	ii
Map symbols	iii
Route-planning map	iv
Distance chart	1
Road atlas	2-45
Index and city environs plans	46-60

Barcelona	47	Porto	55
Lisboa	52	San Sebastián	57
Madrid	53	Sevilla	58

2nd edition February 1998
1st edition February 1996

© The Automobile Association 1998

The Automobile Association retains the copyright in the original edition © 1996 and in all subsequent editions, reprints and amendments to editions listed above.

Published by AA Publishing (a trading name of Automobile Association Developments Limited, whose registered office is Norfolk House, Priestley Road, Basingstoke, Hampshire RG24 9NY. Registered number 1878835).

Mapping produced by the Cartographic Department of The Automobile Association. This atlas has been compiled and produced from the Automaps database utilising electronic and computer technology.

ISBN 0 7495 1759 X

A CIP catalogue for this book is available from The British Library.

Printed in Great Britain by BPC Waterlow Ltd, Dunstable.

The contents of this atlas are believed to be correct at the time of printing. Nevertheless, the publishers cannot be held responsible for any errors or omissions, or for changes in the details given. They would welcome information to help keep this atlas up to date; please write to the Cartographic Editor, Publishing Division, The Automobile Association, Norfolk House, Priestley Road, Basingstoke, Hampshire RG24 9NY.

map pages

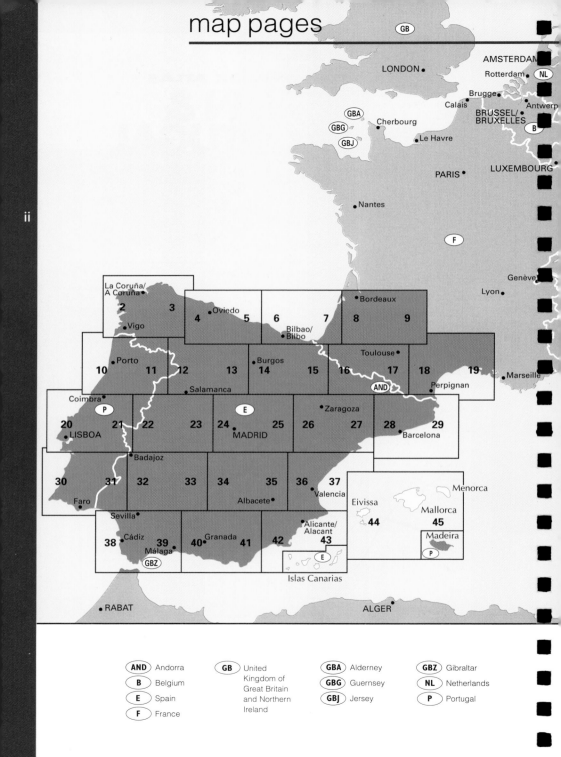

ii

AND	Andorra	
B	Belgium	
E	Spain	
F	France	

GB	United Kingdom of Great Britain and Northern Ireland

GBA	Alderney
GBG	Guernsey
GBJ	Jersey

GBZ	Gibraltar
NL	Netherlands
P	Portugal

map symbols

Toll motorways

 Dual carriageway with road numbers

Single carriageway

 Interchange

Restricted interchange

Service area

Under construction

Non-toll motorways

 Dual carriageway with road numbers

Single carriageway

Interchange

Restricted interchange

Service area

Under construction

National roads

SS45 Dual carriageway with road number

Single carriageway

Regional roads

SS45 Dual carriageway with road number

Single carriageway

Local roads

SS453 Dual carriageway with road number

Single carriageway

D28 Minor road with road number

 Page overlap and number

Symbols

E55 **E55** European international network numbers

╞═════╡ Motorway in tunnel

╞══════╡ Road in tunnel

▬▬ ▬▬ ▬▬ Road under construction

 Toll point

▼ 24 ▼ Distances in kilometres

≫ Gradient 14% and over

> Gradient 6%-13%

 Mountain pass with closure period

Furkapass
2431
3970
▲
EIGER Spot height (metres)

Ferry route (all year)

Hovercraft (all year)

Airport (International)

╞╪╪╪╪╪╪╪╪╡ Car transporter (rail)

Mountain railway

Motor racing circuit

Viewpoint (180° or 360°)

Urban area

Town location

Canal

Wooded area

Boundaries

International

National

Unrecognised international

Restricted frontier crossing

iii

scale

1:1 000 000

10 kilometres : 1 centimetre

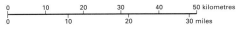

16 miles : 1 inch

LONDON
GB
Southampton
Plymouth
Portsmouth
Dover
Calais
Oostende
Lille
GBA
GBG
GBJ
Cherbourg
Le Havre
Amiens
Rouen
Caen
Brest
St Malo
PARIS
Rennes
Le Mans
Orléans
Nantes
Tours
Bourges
F
Limoges
Clermont-Ferrand
Bordeaux
La Coruña/A Coruña
Oviedo
Santander
San Sebastián/Donostia
Bilbao/Bilbo
Pau
Toulouse
Vigo
Pamplona/Iruñea
Burgos
Porto
Valladolid
Andorra la Vella
AND
Perpignan
Salamanca
Zaragoza
Barcelona
P
E
MADRID
LISBOA
Mérida
Valencia
Menorca
Palma
Mallorca
Eivissa
Albacete
Córdoba
Lagos
Faro
Sevilla
Alicante
Murcia
Cádiz
Granada
Málaga
GBZ
Gibraltar
Tanger
ALGER
Ouahran
RABAT

Tabla de distancias

Ciudad Real - San Sebastián/Donostia = 685km

Leyenda de ciudades (diagonal):

- Albacete (E)
- Alicante/Alacant (E)
- Andorra la Vella (AND)
- Badajoz (E)
- Barcelona (E)
- Bilbao/Bilbo (F)
- Bordeaux (F)
- Burgos (E)
- Cádiz (E)
- Ciudad Real (E)
- Coimbra (P)
- Córdoba (E)
- Cuenca (E)
- Faro (P)
- Gibraltar (GBZ)
- Granada (E)
- La Coruña/A Coruña (E)
- Lagos (P)
- León (E)
- Lisboa (P)
- Madrid (E)
- Málaga (E)
- Mérida (E)
- Murcia (E)
- Nantes (F)
- Oviedo (E)
- Pamplona/Iruñea (E)
- Paris (F)
- Perpignan (F)
- Porto (P)
- Salamanca (E)
- San Sebastián/Donostia (E)
- Santander (E)
- Sevilla (E)
- Toledo (E)
- Toulouse (F)
- Valencia (E)
- Valladolid (E)
- Vigo (E)
- Zaragoza (E)

Matriz de distancias (lectura triangular, cada fila indica las distancias desde esa ciudad a las anteriores):

Alicante/Alacant (E)	166
Andorra la Vella (AND)	688 711
Badajoz (E)	603 554 1026
Barcelona (E)	531 192 1031
Bilbao/Bilbo (F)	643 809 547 609
Bordeaux (F)	996 430 1028 654 334
Burgos (E)	495 661 612 557 618 152 475
Cádiz (E)	634 744 342 1164 1056 1379 908
Ciudad Real (E)	200 366 409 898 731 596 919 448 454
Coimbra (P)	795 961 1156 342 1171 705 1028 557 660 739
Córdoba (E)	371 537 740 1059 278 902 794 646 263 189 622
Cuenca (E)	168 334 559 740 560 584 550 873 402 245 701 535
Faro (P)	717 827 1405 388 1248 1140 1463 992 707 481 346 789 458
Gibraltar (GBZ)	367 622 1332 471 1175 1071 1394 923 147 535 303 720 257
Granada (E)	881 1047 1156 767 1128 612 944 512 1086 825 435 789 906 1055
La Coruña/A Coruña (E)	786 896 1473 390 1316 1208 1531 1060 398 604 415 857 84 1214 1055
Lagos (P)	604 770 509 809 343 666 193 806 550 509 857 415 527 462 530 909
León (E)	829 995 1407 226 1413 947 1270 799 526 635 205 504 312 655 658 632 314 899
Lisboa (P)	256 422 628 396 634 388 711 240 668 522 403 163 751 681 435 820 608 333 632
Madrid (E)	492 1201 432 1044 941 1264 793 262 405 750 173 590 129 126 895 616 550 616 622
Málaga (E)	553 719 978 67 982 740 1063 592 319 396 404 255 510 402 447 451 830 388 487 347 409
Mérida (E)	149 86 796 755 639 795 1083 647 673 945 320 756 457 320 551 305 126 452 830 388 421 408
Murcia (E)	1298 1329 756 1360 979 666 280 807 1713 1251 1360 1447 625 872 636 1013 1150 867 904 307 457 1019 603 968
Nantes (F)	728 894 849 625 912 305 637 315 922 674 922 1113 207 1126 1015 904 122 398 791 1265 122 457 880 1739 1223
Oviedo (E)	698 686 524 760 483 181 312 207 1113 1505 1614 1703 1459 2051 1980 1530 1252 880 1734 398 1856 1850 1649 1297 386
Pamplona/Iruñea (E)	1552 1654 1010 1614 1133 564 1061 1967 1341 1346 1614 1076 758 1424 1349 1103 1253 984 1567 2119 1567 1219 813 808 775 929
Paris (F)	705 729 167 1206 208 643 449 792 449 1070 717 246 626 392 699 736 465 658 701 198 984 1103 1156 946 386 775 898
Perpignan (F)	837 1003 1208 454 1213 747 1070 599 772 608 314 289 636 570 404 404 856 862 318 394 701 198 553 211 289 775 386 621
Porto (P)	484 650 855 311 795 246 394 717 246 1148 448 1070 829 856 570 404 1049 636 553 465 1030 773 289 477 1402 949 314 449 1035
Salamanca (E)	732 773 451 795 569 101 239 241 1148 632 682 185 140 311 640 885 311 915 711 198 1072 1036 829 660 971 404 831 548 670 449
San Sebastián/Donostia (E)	679 845 649 682 712 105 437 184 1094 830 140 587 582 207 252 255 963 275 683 711 517 862 989 831 210 86 516 620 484 862 352
Santander (E)	511 621 1198 219 1041 933 1256 785 123 329 537 185 354 140 207 963 275 915 255 963 289 403 403 543 213 989 989 831 318 989 862 353 837
Sevilla (E)	242 408 697 361 702 466 789 318 619 121 545 354 185 702 632 212 1139 357 687 412 771 71 687 1015 1121 1588 550 550 196 988 799 485 484 1022
Toledo (E)	907 930 188 1137 244 443 409 244 1490 1028 584 895 960 1226 1574 1503 1257 981 1642 1373 820 775 1379 703 539 1465 703 1465 1171 830 977 1023 1216 877 1216
Toulouse (F)	182 175 522 753 365 623 809 515 817 1137 895 382 553 225 901 795 549 981 641 139 706 969 565 139 497 917 357 261 332 497 332 421 261 1186 825 548
Valencia (E)	465 631 738 428 743 277 600 129 725 382 428 609 373 428 918 887 641 451 818 670 194 756 406 332 97 117 332 367 470 427 438 151 470 332 1321 367 1321
Valladolid (E)	880 1046 1141 605 1146 532 680 1003 272 824 883 532 787 743 1051 1055 1589 438 745 469 607 1013 667 1335 735 1321 589 770 151 606 438 735 438 1589 1321 770 770 427
Vigo (E)	430 510 307 722 312 489 303 311 983 521 865 719 334 865 996 866 750 503 822 323 1135 866 948 594 819 606 177 262 487 907 554 262 907 1075 487 262 554 487 177
Zaragoza (E)	166 711 603 531 643 996 495 634 200 795 371 168 717 367 881 786 604 829 256 492 553 149 1298 728 698 1552 705 837 484 732 679 511 242 907 930 182 465 880 430

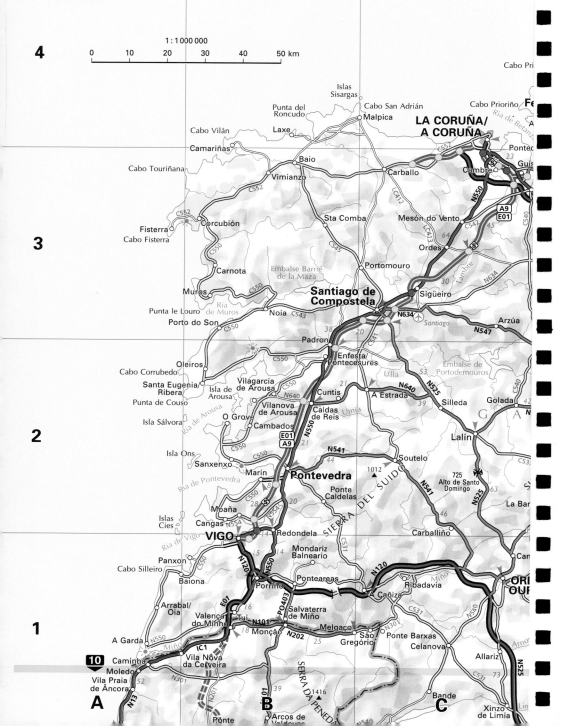

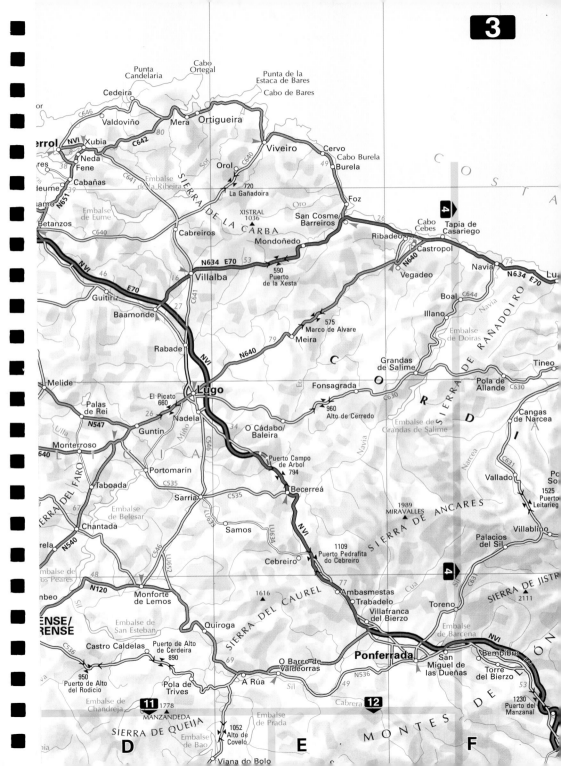

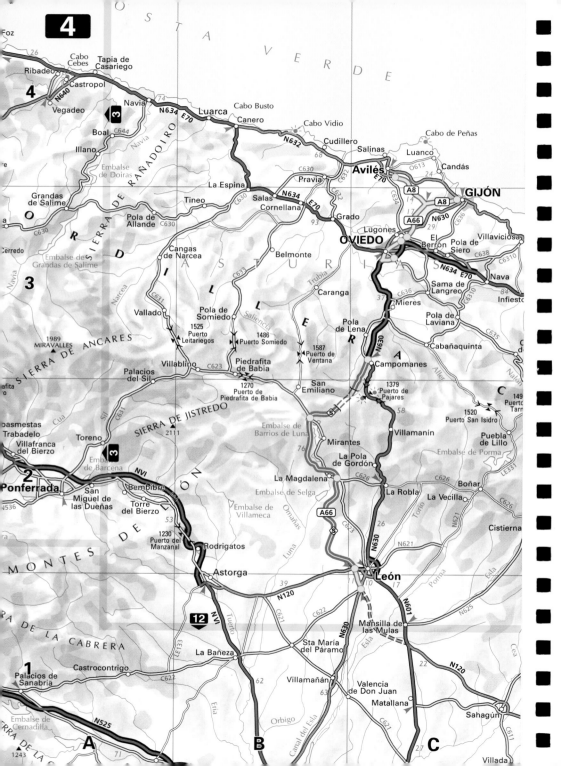

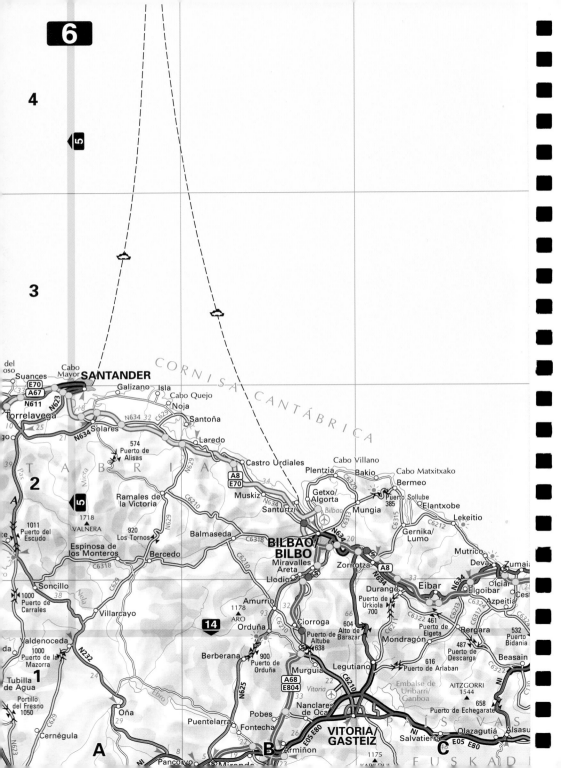

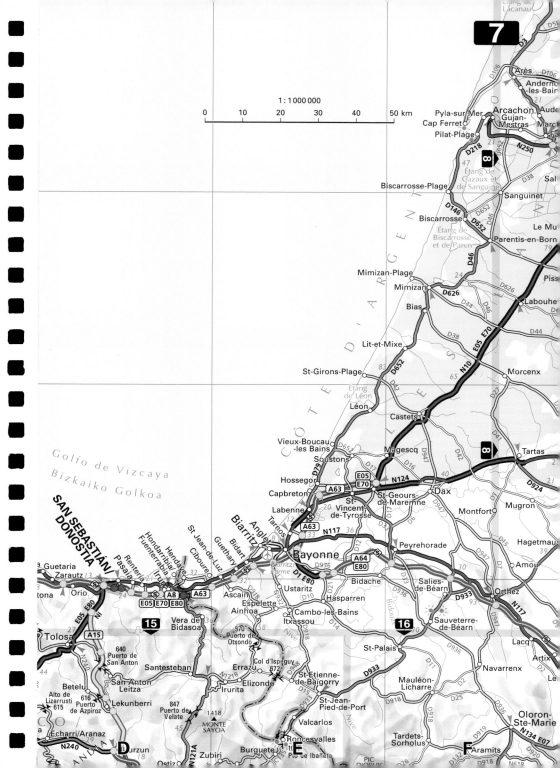

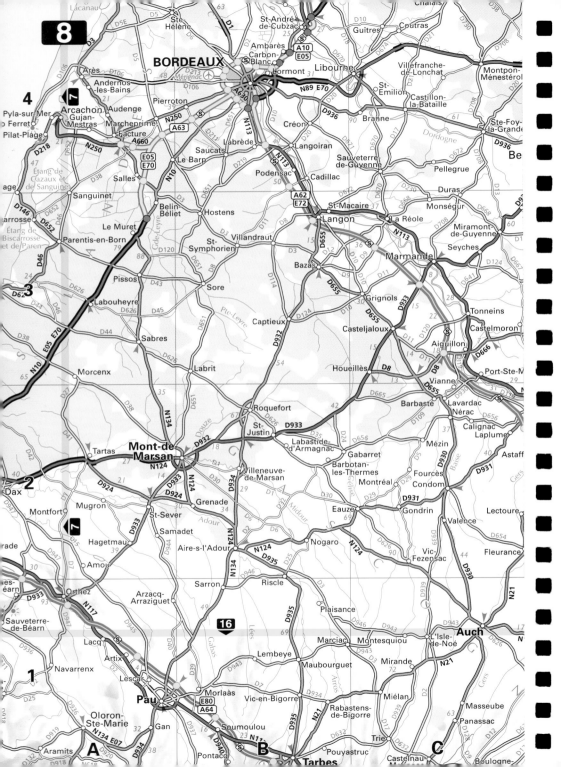

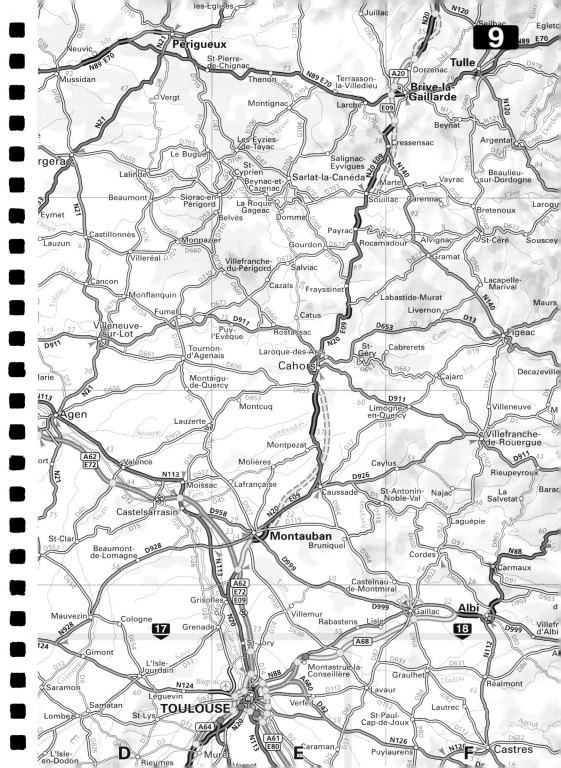

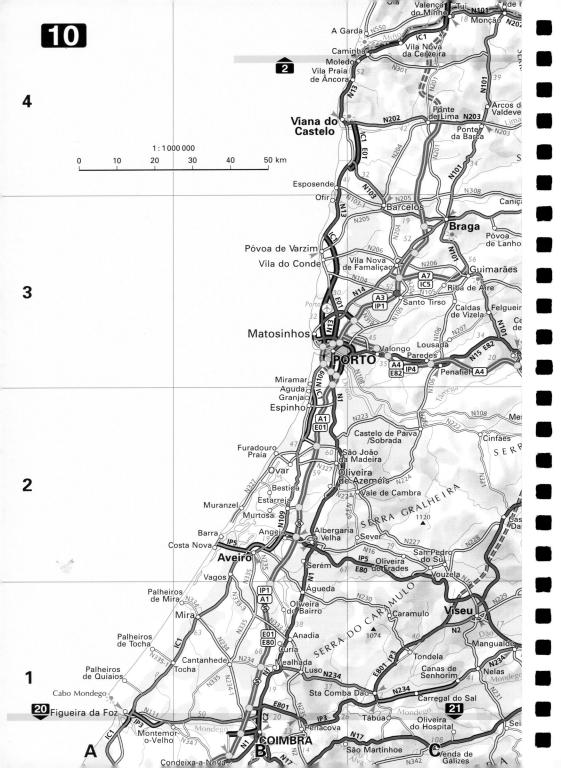

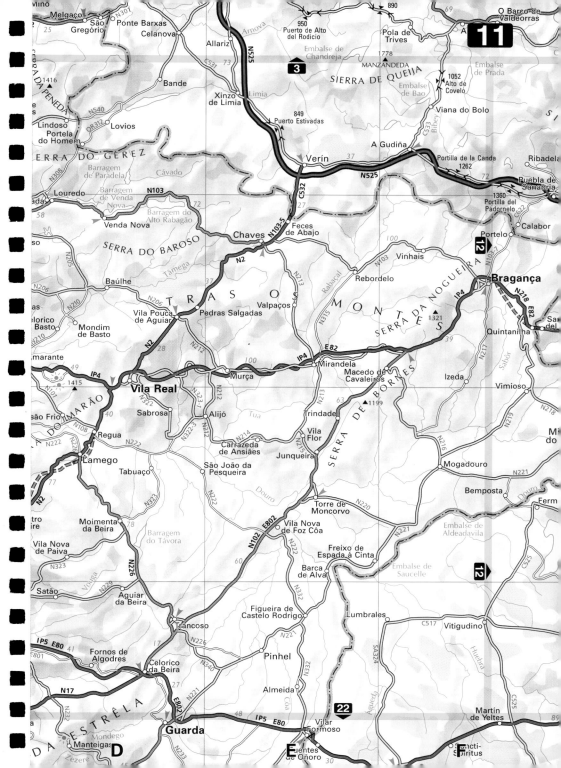

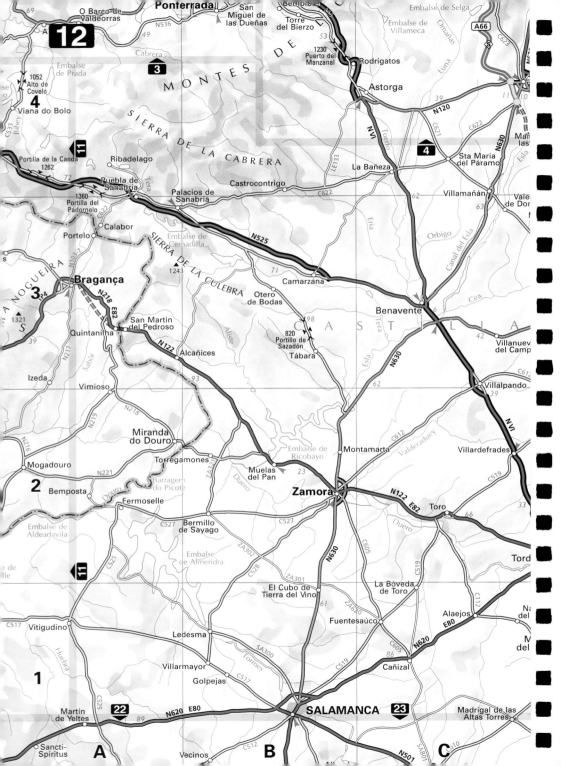

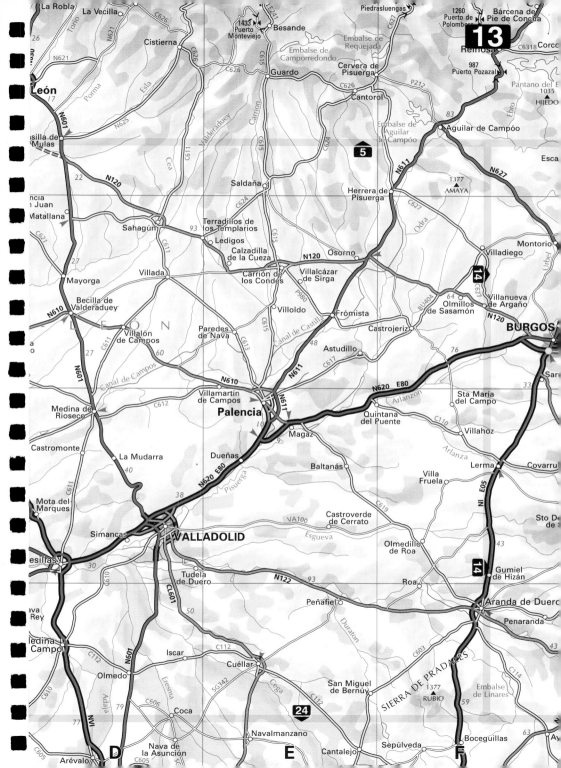

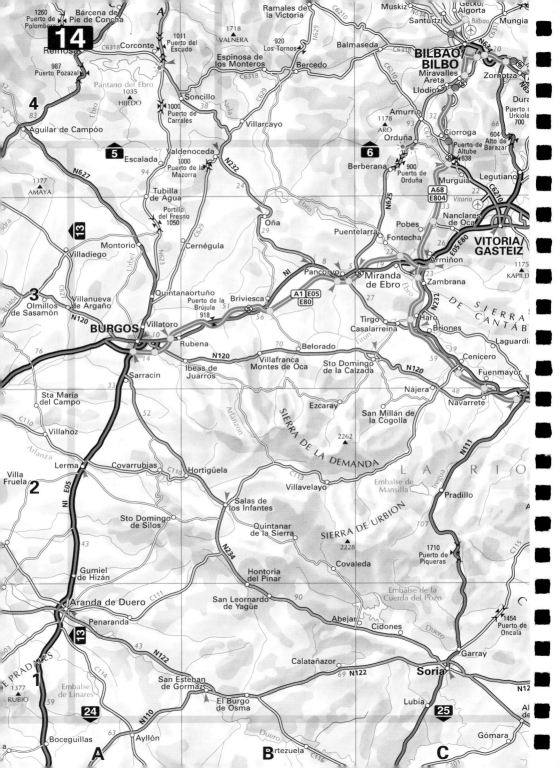

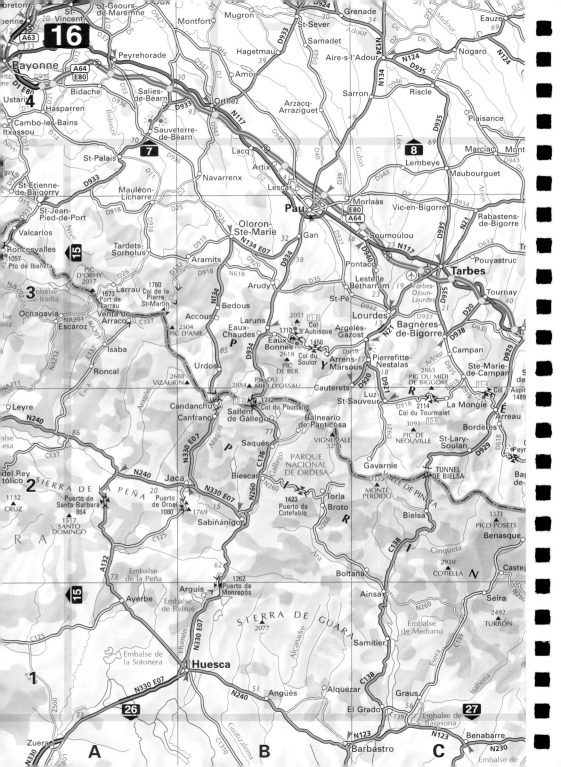

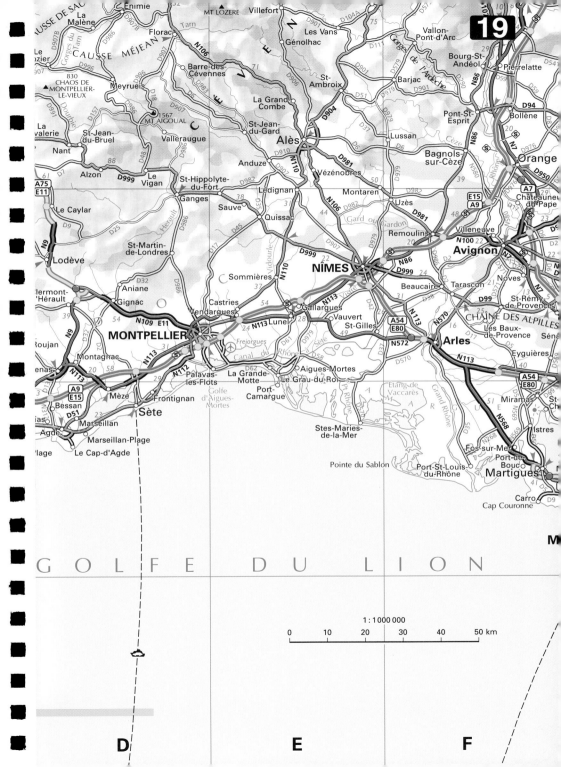

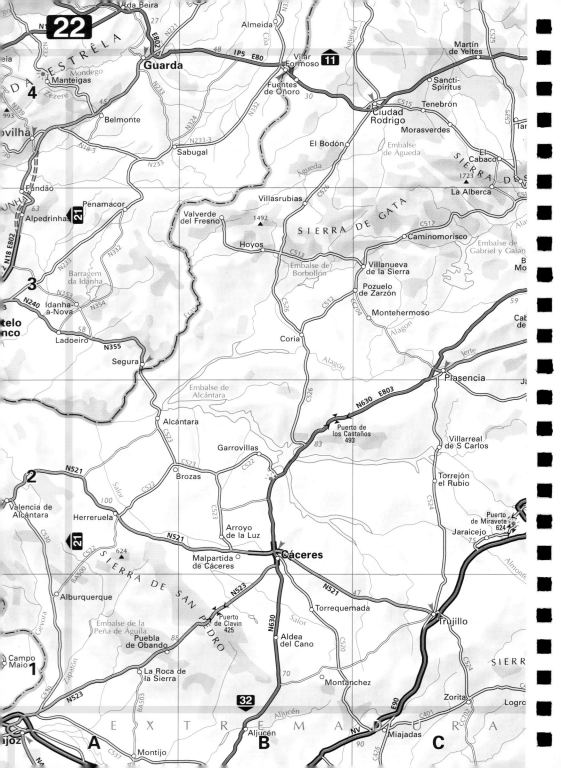

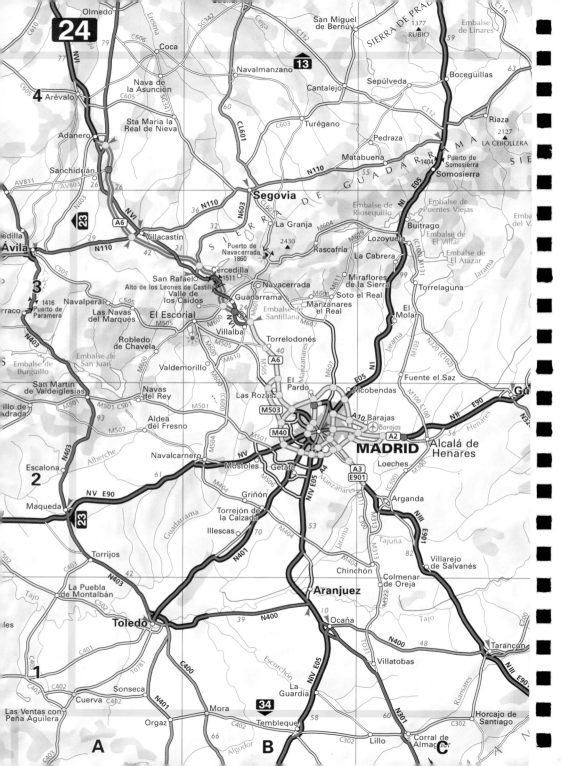

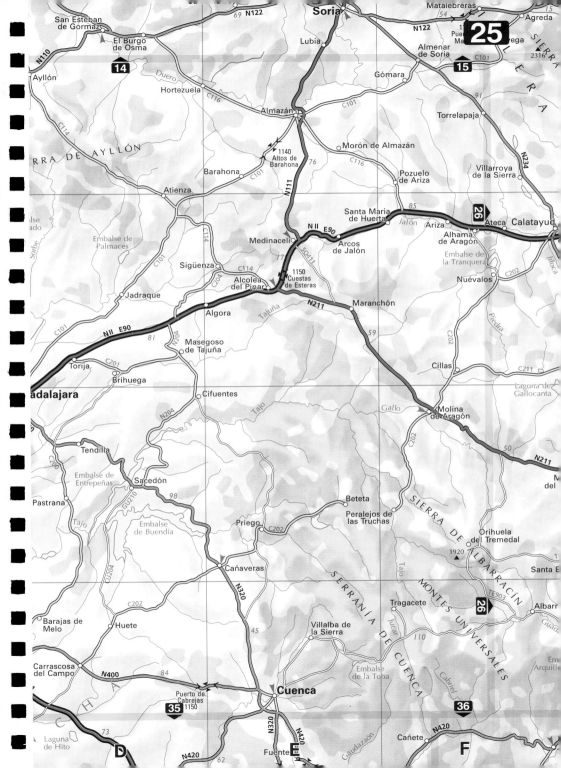

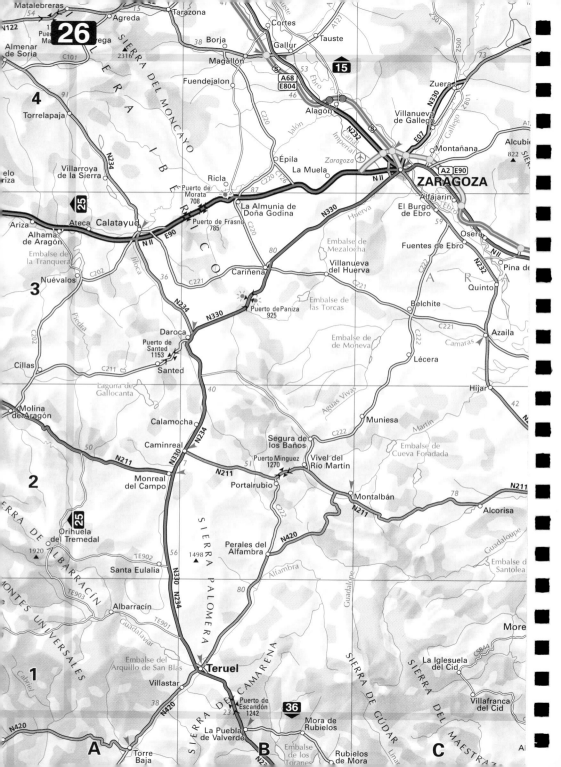

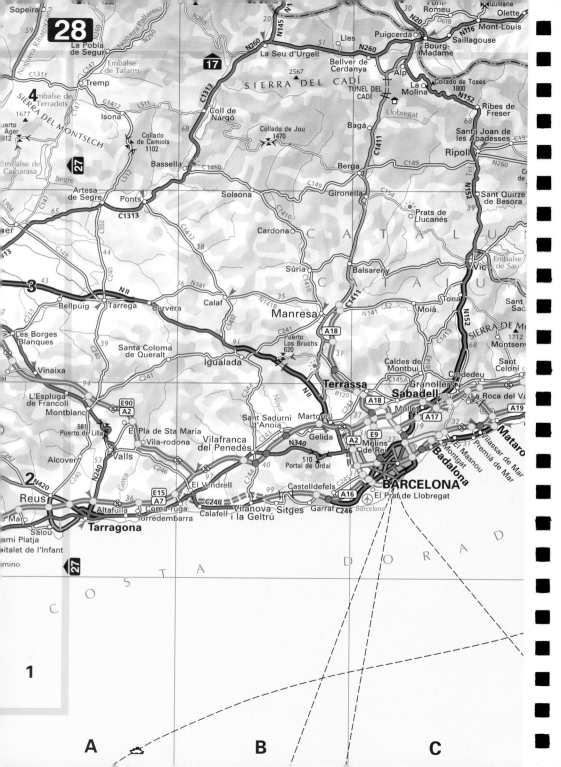

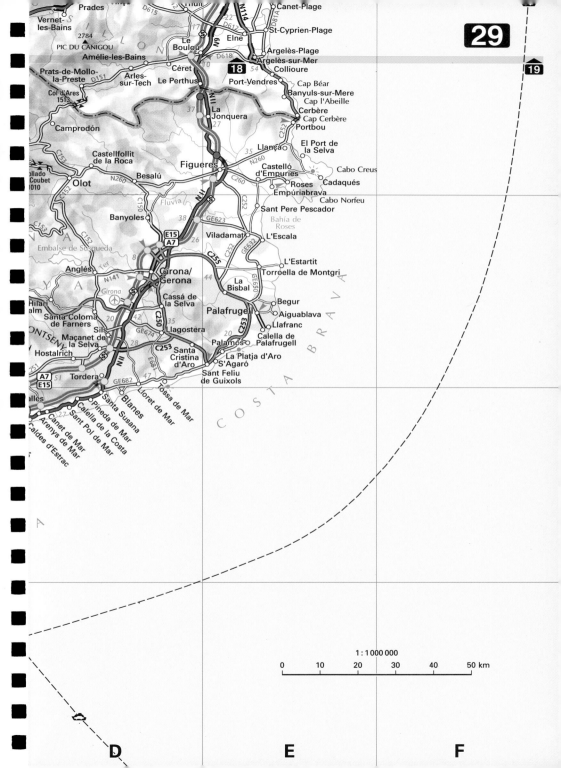

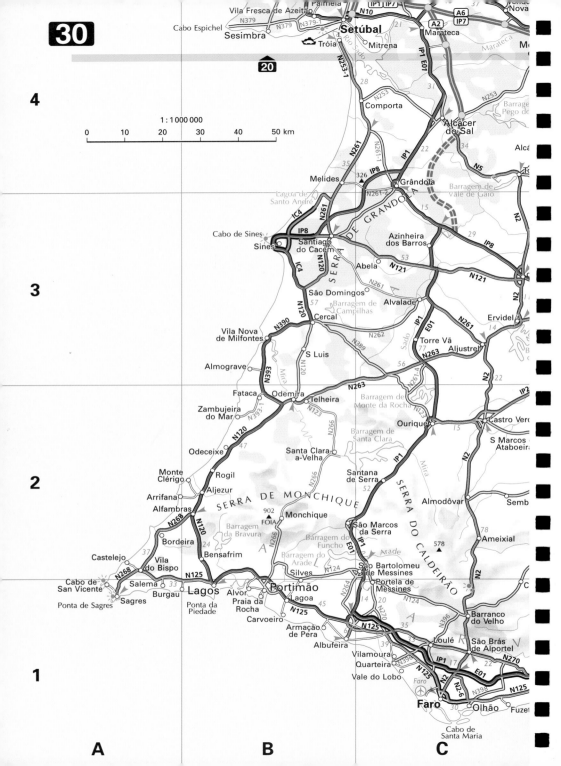

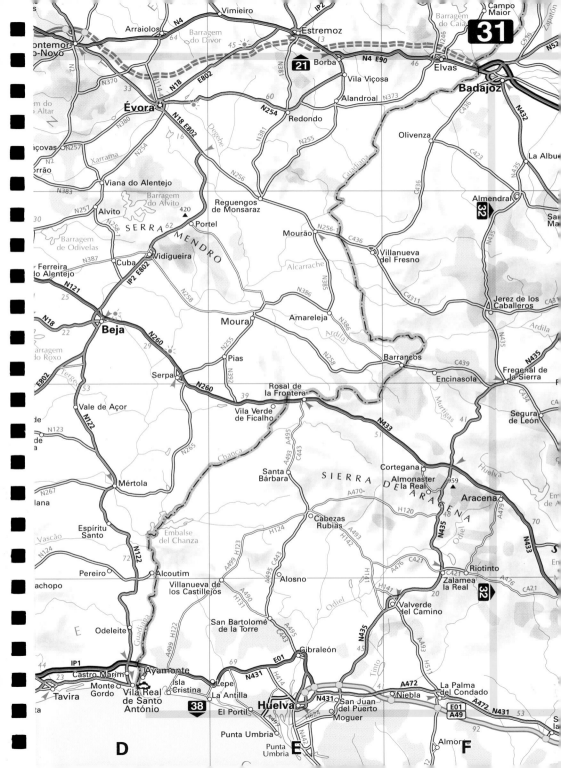

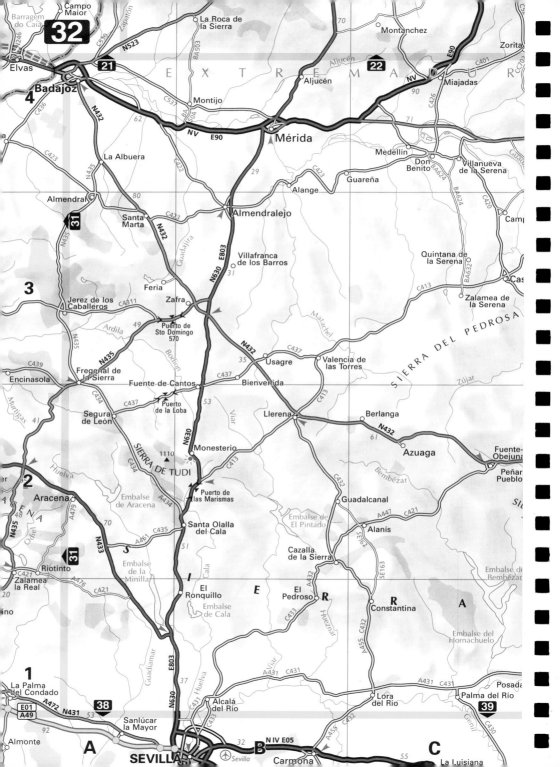

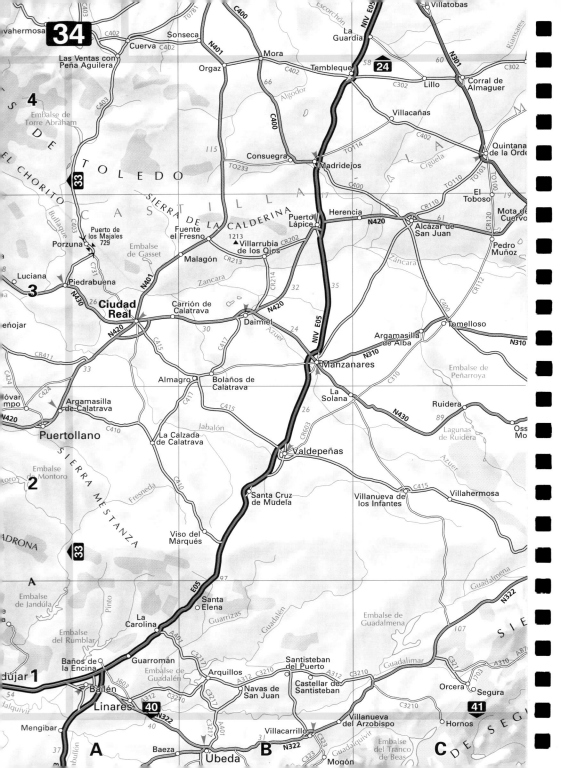

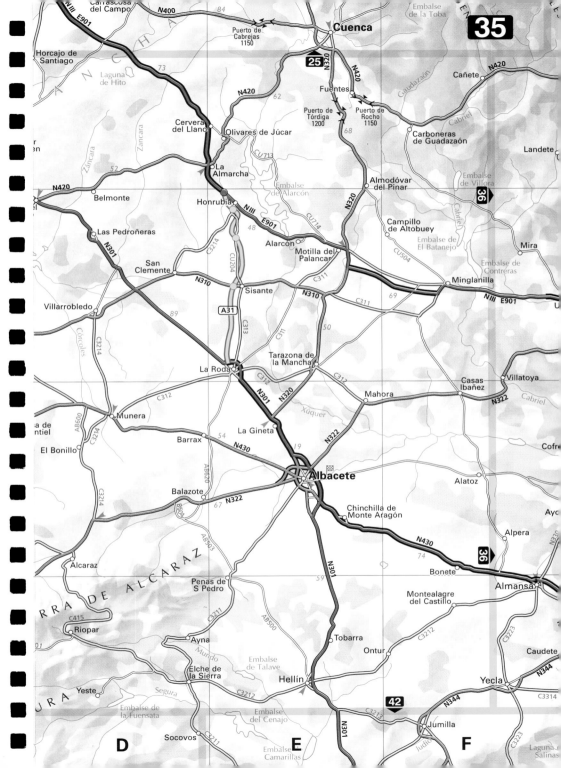

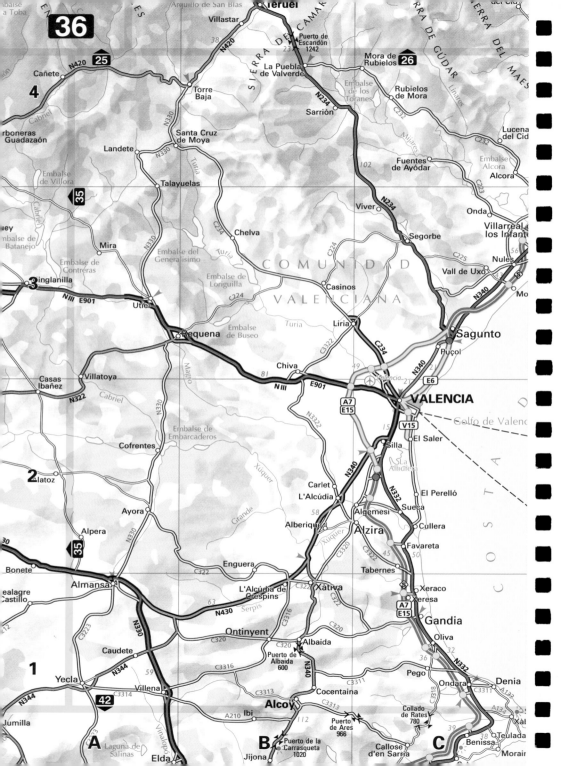

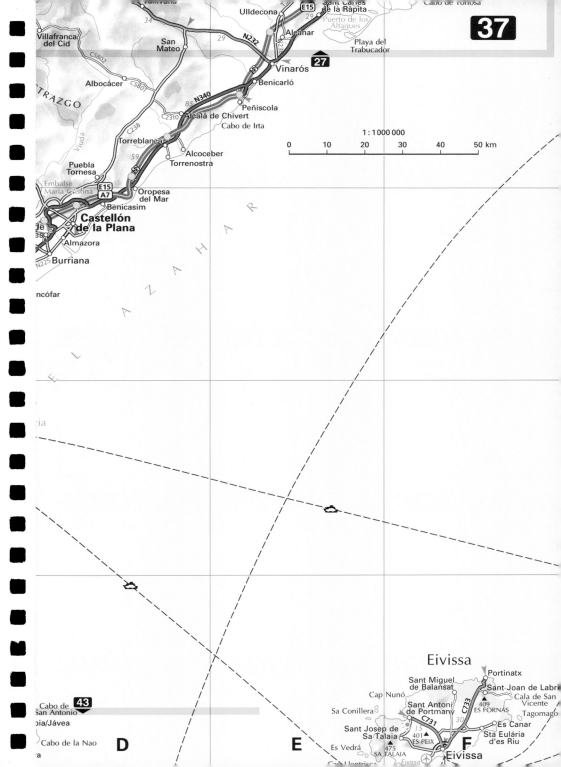

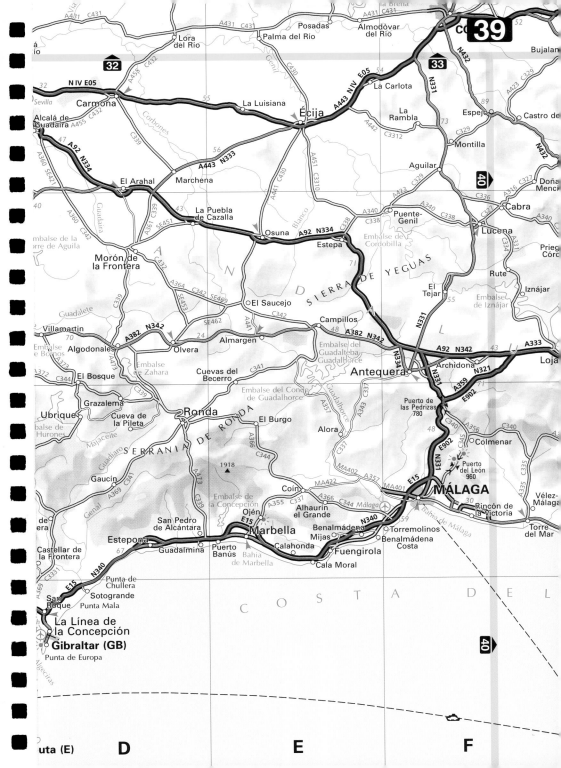

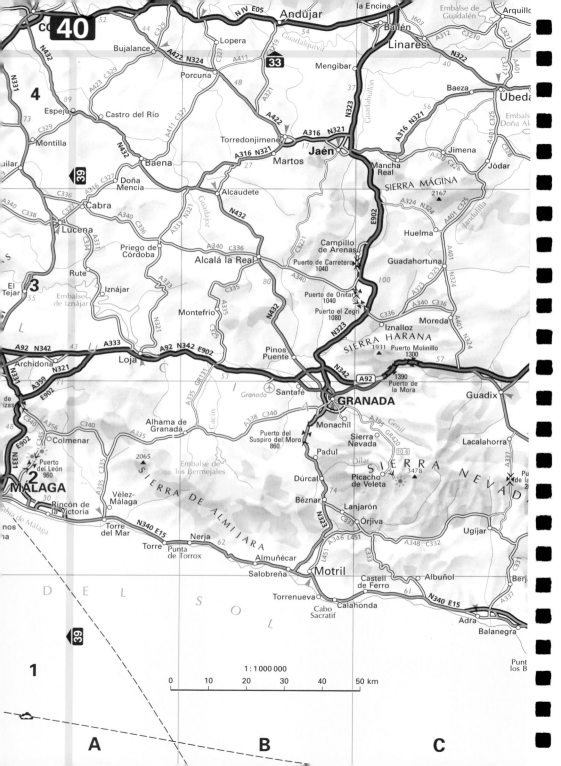

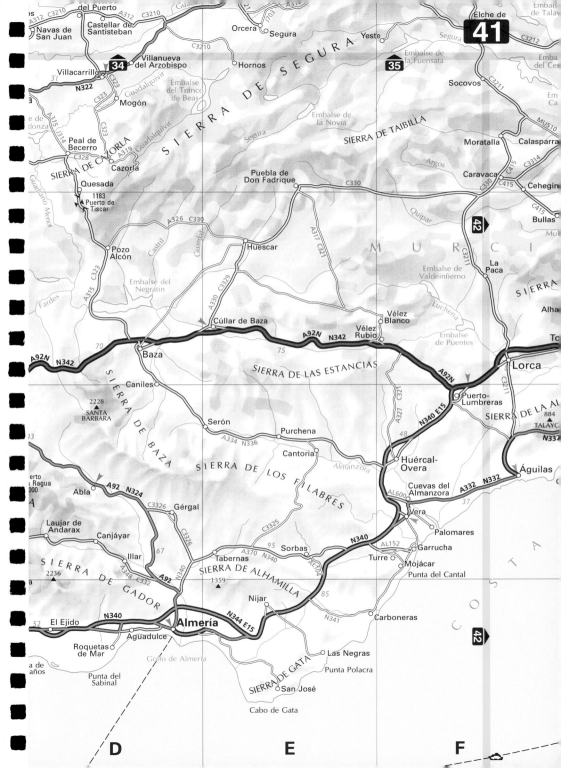

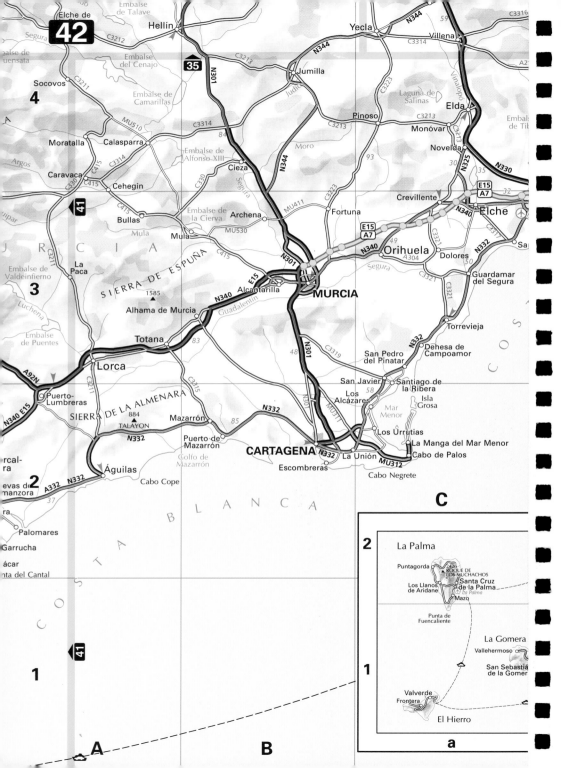

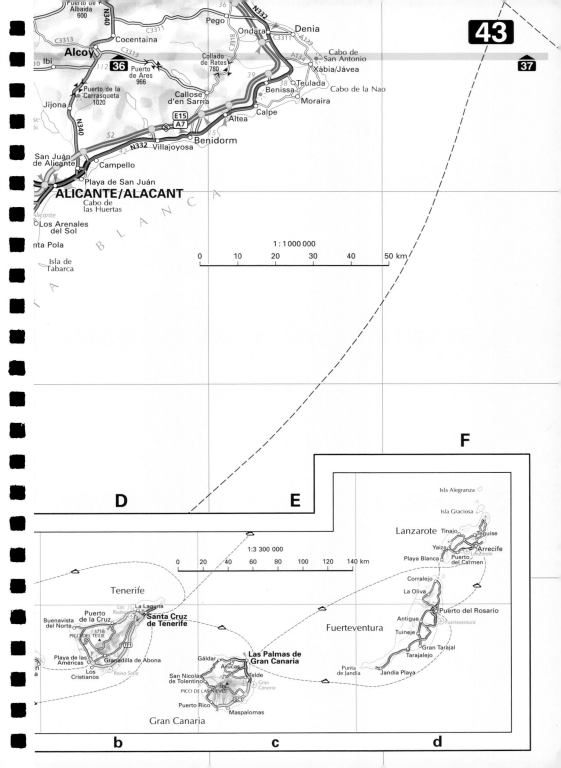

Puerto de Albaida 600

N340

Pego

Ondara

Denia

N332

Alcoy

Cocentaina

C3311

A122

Cabo de San Antonio

C3313

Collado de Rates 780

A134

Xàbia/Jávea

112 **36** Puerto de Ares 966

Callose d'en Sarria

Benissa

Teulada

Cabo de la Nao

Puerto de la Carrasqueta 1020

Moraira

Jijona

N340

Altea

Calpe

52

E15 A7

S

Benidorm

N332 Villajoyosa

San Juán de Alicante

Campello

Playa de San Juán

ALICANTE/ALACANT

Cabo de las Huertas

Alicante

COSTA BLANCA

Los Arenales del Sol

nta Pola

Isla de Tabarca

1 : 1 000 000

0   10   20   30   40   50 km

F

D   **E**

Isla Alegranza

Isla Graciosa

Lanzarote   Tinajo   Teguise

Yaiza   Arrecife

Lanzarote

Playa Blanca   Puerto del Carmen

1:3 300 000

0   20   40   60   80   100   120   140 km

Corralejo

La Oliva

Tenerife

Puerto del Rosario

Los Rodeos   La Laguna

Buenavista del Norte   Puerto de la Cruz   **Santa Cruz de Tenerife**

Antigua   Fuerteventura

PICO DEL TEIDE   3718

Fuerteventura

Tuineje

TF1

Playa de las Américas   Granadilla de Abona

Gran Tarajal

Los Cristianos

Gáldar

Tarajalejo

Reina Sofía

Las Palmas de Gran Canaria

Jandía Playa

na

Arucas   Telde

Punta de Jandía

San Nicolás de Tolentino

PICO DE LAS NIEVES

Gran Canaria

Puerto Rico

GC1

Maspalomas

Gran Canaria

b   **c**   **d**

4

3

2

1

A   B   C

Mallorca

S

Port
de Sóller

Fornalut

Banyalbufar   Sóller

O Valldemo

Sa   Sa
Dragonera   ▲1025   M
GALATZÓ

Pdrt d'Andratx   Andratx   **PALMA**
Cap de Sa Mola   24   PM1
Peguera   C19

Magaluf   Palma
Nova   S'Arenal
Badia de Palma

Cap de   Cap
Cala Figuera   Enderrocat   Cap
Blanc

Eivissa

Portinatx
Sant Miguel
de Balansat   Sant Joan de Labritjá
Cap Nunó   409   Cala de San
Sant Antoni   ES FORNÁS   Vicente
de Portmany   C733   Tagomagó
Sa Conillera   C731
Sant Josep de   401   Es Canar
Sa Talaia   ES PEIX   Sta Eulária
Es Vedrá   475   d'es Riu
Cap Llentrisca   SA TALAIA
Eivissa   **Eivissa**

Punta de ses Portes
S'Espalmador   S'Espardell
Punta de Sa Pedrera
Sant Françesc   Formentera
de Formentera
Cap de Barbaria   192   Punta de Sa Creu
LA MOLA   Punta Roja

I S L A S

1:1 300 000

0   10   20   30   40   50   60 km

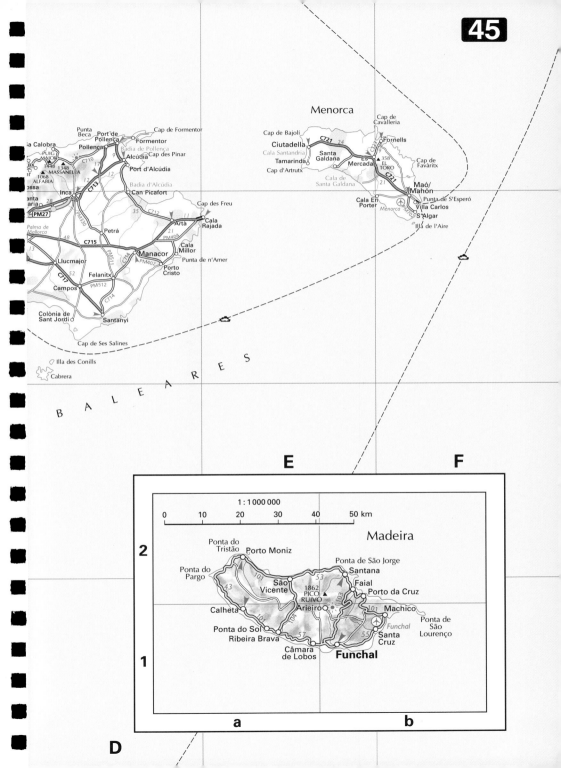

A

A Cañiza E 2 C1
A Coruña/La Coruña E 2 C4
A Estrada E 2 C2
A Garda E 2 A1
A Gudiña E 11 F4
A Rúa E 3 E1
Abejar E 14 C1
Abela P 30 C3
Abeñojar E 33 F3
Abla E 41 D2
Abrantes P 21 D2
Accous F 16 B3
Adanero E 24 A4
Adra E 40 C1
Agde E 19 D2
Agen F 9 D2
Agoncillo E 15 D2
Agreda E 15 D1
Aguadulce E 41 D1
Aguda P 10 B2
Agudo E 33 E3
Águeda P 10 B1
Aguiar da Beira P 11 D1
Aguilar E 39 F4
Aguilar de Campóo E 5 E1
Águilas E 42 A2
Aiguablava E 29 E3
Aigues-Mortes F 19 E3
Aiguillon F 8 C3
Ainhoa F 7 E1
Ainsa E 16 C1
Aire-sur-l'Adour F 8 B2
Alacant/Alicante E 43 D4
Alaejos E 12 C1
Alagón E 26 B4
Alandroal P 31 E4
Alange E 32 B4
Alanís E 32 C2
Alaraz E 23 E4
Alarcón E 35 E3
Alatoz E 35 F2
Alba de Tormes E 23 E4
Albacete E 35 E2
Albaida E 36 B1
Alban F 18 B4
Albarracín E 26 A1
Albergaria a Velha P 10 B2
Alberique E 36 B2
Albi F 9 F1
Albocácer E 37 D4
Albufeira P 30 B1
Albuñol E 40 C1
Alburquerque E 21 F1
Alcácer do Sal P 30 C4
Alcáçovas P 31 D4
Alcalá de Chivert E 37 D4
Alcalá de Guadaira E 39 D4
Alcalá de Henares E 24 C2
Alcalá de los Gazules E 38 C2
Alcalá del Río E 32 B1
Alcalá la Real E 40 B3
Alcanar E 27 E1
Alcanede P 20 C3
Alcanena P 20 C3
Alcañices E 12 A3
Alcañiz E 27 D2
Alcántara E 22 A2
Alcantarilla E 42 B3
Alcaracejos E 33 D2

Alcaraz E 35 D2
Alcarrás E 27 E3
Alcaudete E 40 B3
Alcázar de San Juan E 34 C3
Alcobaça P 20 C3
Alcobendas E 24 B2
Alcoceber E 37 D4
Alcochete P 20 B1
Alcolea del Pinar E 25 E3
Alcora E 36 C4
Alcorisa E 26 C2
Alcoutim P 31 D2
Alcover E 28 A2
Alcoy E 36 B1
Alcubierre E 27 D4
Alcúdia E 45 D4
Aldea del Cano E 22 B1
Aldea del Fresno E 24 A2
Alés F 19 E4
Alfajarín E 26 C3
Alfambras P 30 B2
Alfaro E 15 E2
Alfarràs E 27 E3
Alfeizerão P 20 C3
Algeciras E 38 C1
Algemesí E 36 C2
Algodonales E 39 D3
Algora E 25 E3
Algorta/Getxo E 6 B2
Alhama de Aragón E 25 F3
Alhama de Granada E 40 B2
Alhama de Murcia E 42 B3
Alhaurín el Grande E 39 E2
Alicante / Alacant E 43 D4
Alijó P 11 E2
Aljezur P 30 B2
Aljubarrota P 20 C3
Aljucén E 32 B4
Aljustrel P 30 C3
Allariz E 2 C1
Almacelles E 27 E3
Almadén E 33 E3
Almagro E 34 B3
Almansa E 36 A1
Almargen E 39 E3
Almazán E 25 E4
Almazora E 37 D3
Almeida P 11 E1
Almeirim P 20 C2
Almenar de Soria E 25 F4
Almendral E 32 A3
Almendralejo E 32 B3
Almería E 41 D1
Almodôvar P 30 C2
Almodóvar del Campo E 33 F2
Almodóvar del Pinar E 35 E4
Almodóvar del Río E 33 D1
Almograve P 30 B3
Almonaster la Real E 31 F2
Almonte E 38 B4
Almuñécar E 40 B2
Alora E 39 E2
Alosno E 31 E2
Alp E 28 C4
Alpalhão P 21 E2
Alpedrinhas P 21 F3
Alpera E 36 A2
Alquézar E 16 B1
Alsasua E 15 D3
Altafulla E 28 A2
Altea E 43 E4
Alter do Chão P 21 E2
Alvalade P 30 C3
Alvignac F 9 F3

Alvito P 31 D3
Alvor P 30 B1
Alzira E 36 C2
Alzon F 19 D4
Alzonne F 18 A3
Amarante P 10 C3
Amareleja P 31 E3
Ambarès F 8 B4
Ambasmestas E 3 E1
Ameixial P 30 C2
Amélie-les-Bains F 29 D4
Amou F 8 A2
Amposta E 27 E1
Amurria E 6 B1
Anadia P 10 B1
Andernos-les-Bains F 8 A4
Andorra la Vella AND 17 E1
Andratx E 44 C3
Andújar E 33 F1
Anduze F 19 E4
Angeja P 10 B2
Anglés E 29 D3
Anglet F 7 E2
Angüés E 16 B1
Aniane F 19 D3
Antequera E 39 F3
Antigua E 43 d1
Aoiz E 15 F3
Aracena E 32 A2
Aramits F 16 B3
Aranaz/Echarri E 15 D3
Aranda de Duero E 13 F1
Aranjuez E 24 B1
Arcachon F 7 F4
Archena E 42 B3
Archidona E 39 F3
Arcos de Jalón E 25 E3
Arcos de la Frontera E 38 C3
Arcos de Valdeves P 10 C4
Arenas E 5 D3
Arenas de San Pedro E 23 E4
Arenys de Mar E 29 D2
Ares E 3 D4
Arès F 8 A4
Areta E 6 B2
Arévalo E 24 A4
Argamasilla de Alba E 34 C3
Argamasilla de Calatrava E 33 F2
Arganda E 24 C2
Arganil P 21 E4
Argelès-Gazost F 16 C3
Argelès-Plage F 18 C1
Argelès-sur-Mer F 18 C1
Argentat F 9 F4
Arguedas E 15 E2
Arguis E 16 B1
Arieiro P 45 B1
Ariza E 25 F3
Arles F 19 F3
Arles-sur-Tech F 29 D4
Armação de Pera P 30 B1
Armiñon E 14 C3
Arnedillo E 15 D2
Arnedo E 15 D2
Arquillos E 34 B1
Arrabal/Oiã E 2 A1
Arraiolos P 21 D1
Arreau F 16 C2
Arrecife E 43 d2
Arrens-Marsous F 16 B3
Arrifana P 30 A2
Arriondas E 5 D3
Arronches P 21 E1
Arroyo de la Luz E 22 B2

Arruda dos Vinhos *P*	20	B2
Artà *E*	45	D3
Artesa de Segre *E*	28	A3
Arties *E*	17	D2
Artix *F*	16	B4
Arucas *E*	43	cI
Arudy *F*	16	B3
Arzacq-Arraziguet *F*	8	AI
Arzúa *E*	2	C3
Ascain *F*	7	EI
Aspet *F*	17	D2
Astaffort *F*	9	D2
Astorga *E*	4	BI
Astudillo *E*	13	E3
Ateca *E*	26	A3
Atienza *E*	25	D3
Auch *F*	8	CI
Audenge *F*	8	A4
Audressein *F*	17	E2
Aulus-les-Bains *F*	17	E2
Aurignac *F*	17	D3
Auterive *F*	17	E3
Aveiras de Cima *P*	20	C2
Aveiro *P*	10	B2
Avignon *F*	19	F3
Ávila *E*	23	F3
Avilés *E*	4	C4
Avis *P*	21	DI

Ax-les-Thermes *F*	17	F2
Axat *F*	18	A2
Ayamonte *E*	31	DI
Ayerbe *E*	16	AI
Ayllón *E*	25	D4
Ayna *E*	35	DI
Ayora *E*	36	A2
Azaila *E*	26	C3
Azambuja *P*	20	C2
Azinheira dos Barros *P*	30	C3
Azpeitia *E*	6	CI
Azuaga *E*	32	C2

B

Baamonde *E*	3	D3
Badajoz *E*	32	A4
Badalona *E*	28	C2
Baena *E*	40	A4
Baeza *E*	40	C4
Bagá *E*	28	C4
Bagnères-de-Bigorre *F*	16	C3
Bagnères-de-Luchon *F*	17	D2
Bagnols-sur-Cèze *F*	19	F4

Bailén *E*	34	AI
Baio *E*	2	B3
Baiona *E*	2	AI
Baixas *F*	18	BI
Bakio *E*	6	C2
Balaguer *E*	27	F3
Balanegra *E*	40	CI
Balazote *E*	35	D2
Baleira/O Cádabo *E*	3	E2
Ballobar *E*	27	E3
Balmaseda *E*	6	B2
Balneario de Panticosa *E*	16	B2
Balsareny *E*	28	B3
Baltanás *E*	13	E2
Bande *E*	11	D4
Baños de la Encina *E*	34	AI
Baños de Montemayor *E*	23	D3
Banyalbufar *E*	44	C4
Banyoles *E*	29	D3
Banyuls-sur-Mer *F*	29	E4
Barahona *E*	25	E4
Barajas *E*	24	C2
Barajas de Melo *E*	25	DI
Barbaste *F*	8	C2
Barbastro *E*	27	E4
Barbate de Franco *E*	38	C2
Barbotan-les-Thermes *F*	8	B2
Barca de Alva *P*	11	E2

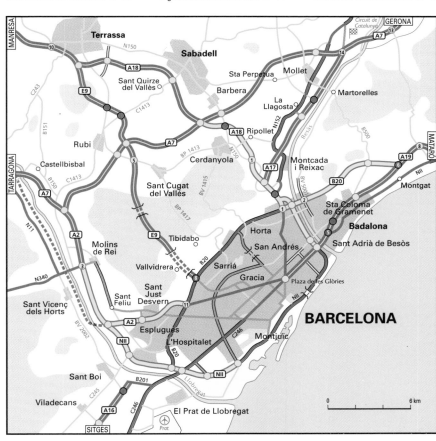

Barcelona E	28	C2
Barcelos P	10	C3
Bárcena de Pie de Concha E	5	F2
Barjac F	19	F4
Barra P	10	B2
Barraco E	23	F3
Barranco do Velho P	30	C1
Barrancos P	31	F3
Barrax E	35	D2
Barre-des-Cévennes F	19	D4
Barreiro P	20	B1
Barreiros/San Cosme E	3	E3
Bassella E	28	B4
Batalha P	20	C3
Baúlhe P	11	D3
Bayonne F	7	E2
Baza E	41	D3
Bazas F	8	B3
Beaucaire F	19	F3
Beaulieu-sur-Dordogne F	9	F4
Beaumont F	9	D3
Beaumont-de-Lomagne F	9	D2
Becerreá E	3	E2
Becilla de Valderaduey E	13	D3
Bédarieux F	18	C3
Bedous F	16	B3
Begur E	29	E3
Beja P	31	D3
Béjar E	23	D3
Belalcázar E	33	D3
Belcaire F	17	F2
Belchite E	26	C3
Belin-Béliet F	8	A3
Bellpuig E	27	F3
Bellver de Cerdanya E	28	C4
Belmont-sur-Rance F	18	C3
Belmonte E	35	D3
Belmonte P	22	A4
Belmonte E	4	B3
Belorado E	14	B3
Belvès F	9	E3
Bembibre E	4	A2
Bemposta P	12	A2
Benabarre E	27	E4
Benalmádena E	39	E2
Benalmádena Costa E	39	E2
Benasque F	16	C2
Benavente P	20	C2
Benavente E	12	C3
Benicarló E	37	E4
Benicasím E	37	D3
Benidorm E	43	D4
Benissa E	43	E4
Bensafrim P	30	B2
Berberana E	14	C4
Bercedo E	6	A2
Berga E	28	C4
Bergara E	6	C1
Bergerac F	9	D4
Berja E	40	C1
Berlanga E	32	C2
Bermeo E	6	C2
Bermillo de Sayago E	12	B2
Besalú E	29	D4
Besande E	5	D2
Bessan F	19	D2
Bestida P	10	B2
Betanzos E	2	C3
Betelu E	15	E3
Beteta E	25	E2
Beynac-et-Cazenac F	9	E4
Beynat F	9	F4
Béziers F	18	C2
Béznar E	40	B2

Biarritz F	7	E2
Bias F	7	F3
Bidache F	7	E2
Bidart F	7	E2
Bielsa E	16	C2
Bienvenida E	32	B3
Biescas E	16	B2
Bilbao/Bilbo E	6	B2
Bilbo/Bilbao E	6	B2
Binéfar E	27	E4
Biscarrosse F	7	F3
Biscarrosse-Plage F	7	F4
Blanes E	29	D2
Boal E	4	A4
Boceguillas E	24	C4
Bolaños de Calatrava E	34	B3
Bollène F	19	F4
Boltaña E	16	C2
Bombarral P	20	B3
Boñar E	4	C2
Bonete E	35	F2
Borba P	31	E4
Bordeaux F	8	B4
Bordeira P	30	A2
Bordères F	16	C2
Borja E	15	E1
Bornos E	38	C3
Bossost E	17	D2
Boulogne-sur-Gesse F	17	D3
Bourg F	8	B4
Bourg-Madame F	17	F1
Bourg-St-Andéol F	19	F4
Boussens F	17	E3
Braga P	10	C3
Bragança P	11	F3
Branne F	8	C4
Brassac F	18	B3
Brazatortas E	33	F2
Bretenoux F	9	F3
Brihuega E	25	D3
Briones E	14	C3
Brive-la-Gaillarde F	9	F4
Briviesca E	14	B3
Broto E	16	B2
Brozas E	22	A2
Bruniquel F	9	E2
Buenavista del Norte E	43	b1
Buitrago E	24	C3
Bujalance E	33	E1
Bujaraloz E	27	D3
Bullas E	42	A3
Burela E	3	E4
Burgau P	30	B1
Burgos E	14	A3
Burguete E	15	F3
Burriana E	37	D3

C

Cabañaquinta E	4	C3
Cabañas E	3	D4
Cabeza del Buey E	33	D3
Cabezas Rubias E	31	E2
Cabezón de la Sal E	5	E2
Cabezuela del Valle E	23	D3
Cabo de Palos E	42	C2
Cabo de San Vicente P	30	A1
Cabra E	40	A3
Cabreiros E	3	D3
Cabrerets F	9	F3

Cabuérniga E	5	E2
Cáceres E	22	B2
Cachopo P	30	C1
Cadaqués E	29	E4
Cadillac F	8	B4
Cádiz E	38	B2
Cahors F	9	E3
Cajarc F	9	F3
Cala En Porter E	45	F3
Cala Millor E	45	D3
Cala Moral E	39	E2
Cala Rajada E	45	E3
Calabor E	12	A3
Calaf E	28	B3
Calafell E	28	B2
Calahonda E	40	B1
Calahonda E	39	E2
Calahorra E	15	D2
Calamocha E	26	B2
Calasparra E	42	A4
Calatañazor E	14	B1
Calatayud E	26	A3
Caldas da Rainha P	20	B3
Caldas de Reis E	2	B2
Caldas de Vizela P	10	C3
Caldes d'Estrac E	29	D2
Caldes de Montbui E	28	C3
Calella de la Costa E	29	D2
Calella de Palafrugell E	29	E3
Calheta P	45	a1
Calignac F	8	C2
Callose d'En Sarria E	43	D4
Calpe E	43	E4
Calzadilla de la Cueza E	13	E3
Câmara de Lobos P	45	a1
Camarès F	18	C3
Camariñas E	2	B4
Camarzana E	12	B3
Cambados E	2	B2
Cambeo E	2	C1
Cambo-les-Bains F	7	E1
Cambre E	2	C3
Cambrils de Mar E	27	F2
Caminha P	2	A1
Caminomorisco E	22	C3
Caminreal E	26	B2
Campan F	16	C3
Campanario E	32	C3
Campello E	43	D4
Campillo de Altobuey E	35	F3
Campillo de Arenas E	40	C3
Campillos E	39	E3
Campo de Caso E	4	C3
Campo Maior P	21	F1
Campodón E	29	D4
Campomanes E	4	C3
Campos E	45	D3
Can Picafort E	45	D3
Canas de Senhorim P	10	C1
Cañaveras E	25	E2
Cancon F	9	D3
Candanchú E	16	B2
Candás E	4	C4
Candasnos E	27	D3
Candeleda E	23	E2
Canero E	4	B4
Canet de Mar E	29	D2
Canet-Plage F	18	C1
Cañete E	35	F4
Canfranc E	16	B2
Cangas E	2	B2
Cangas de Narcea E	4	A3
Cangas de Onis E	5	D3
Caniçada P	11	D3

Caniles E	41 D3	Castries F	19 E3
Cañizal E	12 C1	Castro Caldelas E	3 D1
Canjáyar E	41 D2	Castro Daire P	10 C2
Cantalejo E	24 B4	Castro del Río E	40 A4
Cantanhede P	10 B1	Castro Marim P	31 D1
Cantoria E	41 E2	Castro Urdiales E	6 B2
Cantorol E	5 E1	Castro Verde P	30 C2
Cap Ferret F	7 F4	Castrocontrigo E	12 B4
Capbreton F	7 E2	Castrojeriz E	13 F3
Capendu F	18 B2	Castromonte E	13 D2
Capestang F	18 C2	Castropol E	3 F3
Captieux F	8 B3	Castroverde de Cerrato E	13 E2
Caraman F	17 F3	Castuera E	32 C3
Caramulo P	10 C1	Catus F	9 E3
Caranga E	4 B3	Caudete E	36 A1
Caravaca E	42 A4	Caunes-Minervois F	18 B3
Carballiño E	2 C2	Caussade F	9 E2
Carballo E	2 C3	Cauterets F	16 C3
Carbon-Blanc F	8 B4	Caylus F	9 F2
Carboneras E	41 E1	Cazalla de la Sierra E	32 B2
Carboneras de Guadazaón E	35 F4	Cazals F	9 E3
Carbonne F	17 E3	Cazères F	17 E3
Carcassonne F	18 B2	Cazorla E	41 D4
Carcastillo E	15 E2	Cebreiro E	3 E2
Carcavelos P	20 A2	Cedeira E	3 D4
Cardedeu E	28 C3	Cehegín E	42 A4
Cardona E	28 B3	Celanova E	2 C1
Carennac F	9 F3	Celorico da Beira P	11 D1
Cariñena E	26 B3	Celorico de Basto P	11 D3
Carlet E	36 B2	Cenicero E	14 C3
Carmaux F	9 F2	Cerbère F	29 E4
Carmona E	39 D4	Cercal P	30 B3
Carnota E	2 B3	Cercal P	20 B2
Carrascosa del Campo E	25 D1	Cercedilla E	24 B3
Carrazeda de Ansiães P	11 E2	Céret F	29 D4
Carregado P	20 B2	Cernégula E	14 B3
Carregal do Sal P	10 C1	Cervera E	28 A3
Carrión de Calatrava E	34 A3	Cervera de Pisuerga E	5 E2
Carrión de los Condes E	13 E3	Cervera del Llano E	35 E4
Carro F	19 F2	Cervera del Río Alhama E	15 D1
Cartagena E	42 B2	Cervo E	3 E4
Cartaxó P	20 C2	Cestona E	6 C1
Carvoeiro P	30 B1	Ceuta E	38 C1
Casalarreina E	14 C3	Chalabre F	18 A2
Casas Ibañez E	35 F2	Chamusca P	20 C2
Cascais P	20 A2	Chantada E	3 D2
Casinos E	36 B3	Chão de Codes P	21 D3
Caspe E	27 D2	Châteauneuf-du-Pape F	19 F3
Cassá de la Selva E	29 D3	Chaves P	11 E3
Cassagnes-Bégonhès F	18 B4	Chelva E	36 B3
Castanheira de Pêra P	21 D4	Chiclana de la Frontera E	38 B2
Castejón de Monegros E	27 D3	Chinchilla de Monte Aragón E	35 E2
Castejón de Sos E	16 C2	Chinchón E	24 C2
Castelejo P	30 A2	Chipiona E	38 B3
Casteljaloux F	8 C3	Chiva E	36 B3
Castell de Ferro E	40 C1	Ciboure F	7 D2
Castellar de la Frontera E	39 D2	Cidones E	14 C1
Castellar de Santisteban E	34 B1	Cierp-Gaud F	17 D2
Castelldefels E	28 B2	Cieza E	42 B4
Castellfollit de la Roca E	29 D4	Cifuentes E	25 D2
Castelló d'Empuries E	29 E4	Cillas E	25 F3
Castellón de la Plana E	37 D3	Cinfães P	10 C2
Castelmoron F	8 C3	Cintegabelle F	17 F3
Castelnau-de-Montmiral F	9 F2	Cintruénigo E	15 D1
Castelnau-Magnoac F	17 D3	Ciorroga E	6 B1
Castelnaudary F	18 A3	Cistierna E	5 D2
Castelo Branco P	21 F3	Ciudad Real E	34 A3
Castelo de Paiva/Sobrada P	10 C2	Ciudad Rodrigo E	22 C4
Castelo de Vide P	21 E2	Ciutadella E	45 E4
Castelsarrasin F	9 D2	Clermont-l'Hérault F	19 D3
Castets F	7 F2	Coca E	13 D1
Castillon-la-Bataille F	8 C4	Cocentaina E	36 B1
Castillonnès F	9 D3	Cofrentes E	36 A2
Castres F	18 B3	Coimbra P	21 D4

Coín E	39 E2		
Coina P	20 B1		
Colares P	20 A2		
Coll de Nargó E	28 B4		
Collioure F	29 E4		
Colmenar E	39 F2		
Colmenar de Oreja E	24 C1		
Cologne F	9 D1		
Colònia de Sant Jordi E	45 D3		
Colunga E	5 D3		
Coma-ruga E	28 B2		
Comillas E	5 E3		
Comporta P	30 C4		
Condeixa-a-Nova P	21 D4		
Condom F	8 C2		
Conil de la Frontera E	38 B2		
Constantina E	32 C1		
Consuegra E	34 B4		
Corconte E	5 F2		
Corcurbión E	2 B3		
Cordes F	9 F2		
Córdoba E	33 D1		
Corella E	15 D2		
Coria E	22 B3		
Cornellana E	4 B3		
Corral de Almaguer E	34 C4		
Corralejo E	43 d2		
Cortegana E	31 F2		
Cortes E	15 E1		
Coruche E	20 C2		
Costa da Caparica P	20 B1		
Costa Nova P	10 B2		
Couiza F	18 A2		
Coutras F	8 C4		
Covadonga E	5 D3		
Covaleda E	14 B2		
Covarrubias E	14 A2		
Covilhã P	21 F4		
Crato P	21 E2		
Créon F	8 B4		
Cressensac F	9 F4		
Crevillente E	42 C3		
Cruzamento de Pegões P	20 C1		
Cruzy F	18 C2		
Cuba P	31 D3		
Cudillero E	4 B4		
Cuéllar E	13 E1		
Cuenca E	25 E1		
Cuerva E	24 A1		
Cueva de la Pileta E	39 D2		
Cuevas del Almanzora E	41 F2		
Cuevas del Becerro E	39 E3		
Cúllar de Baza E	41 E3		
Cullera E	36 C2		
Cuntis E	2 B2		
Curia P	10 B1		

D

Daimiel E	34 B3		
Daroca E	26 B3		
Dax F	7 F2		
Dehesa de Campoamor E	42 C3		
Denia E	36 C1		
Deva E	6 C2		
Dolores E	42 C3		
Domme F	9 E3		
Don Benito E	32 C4		
Doña Mencía E	40 A4		
Donostia/San Sebastián E	7 D1		

Donzenac F	9	F4
Donzère F	19	F4
Dos Hermanas E	38	C4
Dueñas E	13	E2
Durango E	6	C1
Duras F	8	C3
Durban-Corbières F	18	B2
Dúrcal E	40	B2

E

Eaux-Bonnes F	16	B3
Eaux-Chaudes F	16	B3
Eauze F	8	C2
Echarri/Aranaz E	15	D3
Écija E	39	E4
Eibar E	6	C1
Eivissa E	44	A3
Ejea de los Caballeros E	15	F1
El Arahal E	39	D4
El Barco de Avila E	23	D3
El Berrón E	4	C3
El Bodón E	22	B4
El Bonillo E	35	D2
El Bosque E	39	D3
El Burgo E	39	E2
El Burgo de Ebro E	26	C3
El Burgo de Osma E	14	B1
El Cabaco E	22	C4
El Cubo de Tierra del Vino E	12	B1
El Ejido E	41	D1
El Escorial E	24	B3
El Grado E	16	C1
El Masnou E	28	C2
El Molar E	24	C3
El Pardo E	24	B2
El Pedroso E	32	B1
El Perelló E	36	C2
El Perelló E	27	E1
El Pla de Sta María E	28	A2
El Pont de Suert E	17	D1
El Port de la Selva E	29	E4
El Portil E	31	E1
El Prat del Llobregat E	28	C2
El Puente del Arzobispo E	23	E2
El Real de San Vicente E	23	F2
El Rocío E	38	B4
El Ronquillo E	32	B1
El Saler E	36	C2
El Saucejo E	39	E3
El Serrat AND	17	E1
El Tejar E	39	F3
El Toboso E	34	C3
El Vendrell E	28	B2
El Villar de Arnedo E	15	D2
Elantxobe E	6	C2
Elche E	42	C3
Elche de la Sierra E	35	D1
Elda E	42	C4
Elgoibar E	6	C1
Elizondo E	15	F4
Elne F	18	B1
Elvas P	31	F4
Empúriabrava E	29	E4
Encamp AND	17	E1
Encinasola E	31	F3
Enfesta/Pontecesures E	2	B2
Enguera E	36	B2
Entronoamento P	21	D3
Épila E	26	B4

Ericeira P	20	B2
Errazu E	15	F4
Erro E	15	E3
Ervidel P	30	C3
Es Canar E	44	B3
Es Mercadal E	45	E4
Escalada E	14	A4
Escalona E	23	F2
Escároz E	15	F3
Escatrón E	27	D3
Escombreras E	42	B2
Espejo E	40	A4
Espelette F	7	E1
Espiel E	33	D2
Espinama E	5	D2
Espinho P	10	B2
Espinosa de los Monteros E	6	A2
Espíritu Santo P	31	D2
Esposende P	10	B4
Espot E	17	D1
Estagel F	18	B1
Estella E	15	D3
Estepa E	39	E3
Estepona E	39	D2
Esterri de Aneu E	17	D2
Estoril P	20	A2
Estremoz P	21	E1
Évora P	31	D4
Eymet F	8	C3
Ezcaray E	14	B2

F

Faial P	45	b2
Falset E	27	E2
Fanjeaux F	18	A2
Faro P	30	C1
Fataca P	30	B2
Fátima P	20	C3
Favareta E	36	C2
Feces de Abajo P	11	E3
Felanitx E	45	D3
Felgueiras P	10	C3
Fene E	3	D4
Feria E	32	A3
Fermoselle E	12	A2
Ferreira do Alentejo P	30	C3
Ferreira do Zêzere P	21	D3
Ferrol E	3	D4
Figeac F	9	F3
Figueira da Foz P	10	A1
Figueira de Castelo Rodrigo P	11	E1
Figueiró dos Vinhos P	21	D3
Figueres E	29	E4
Fisterra E	2	A3
Fitero E	15	D1
Fleurance F	9	D2
Flix E	27	E2
Florac F	19	D4
Foix F	17	F2
Fonsagrada E	3	E2
Font-Romeu F	17	F1
Fontecha E	14	C3
Formentor E	45	D4
Fornalutux E	45	D4
Fornells E	45	F4
Fornos de Algodres P	11	D1
Fortuna E	42	B3
Fos F	17	D2
Fos-sur-Mer F	19	F2

Fourcès F	8	C2
Foz E	3	E3
Foz do Arelho P	20	B3
Fraga E	27	E3
Frayssinet F	9	E3
Fregenal de la Sierra E	32	A3
Freixo de Espada à Cinta P	11	E2
Frómista E	13	E3
Fronteira P	21	E1
Frontera E	42	a1
Frontignan F	19	D2
Fuencaliente E	33	E2
Fuendejalon E	26	B4
Fuengirola E	39	E2
Fuenmayor E	14	C3
Fuente Dé E	5	D2
Fuente de Cantos E	32	B2
Fuente el Fresno E	34	B3
Fuente el Saz E	24	C3
Fuente-Obejuna E	32	C2
Fuenterrabía/Hondarribia E	7	D2
Fuentes E	35	E4
Fuentes de Ayódar E	36	C4
Fuentes de Ebro E	26	C3
Fuentes de Oñoro E	22	B4
Fuentesaúco E	12	C1
Fumel F	9	D3
Funchal P	45	b1
Fundão P	21	F3
Furadouro Praia P	10	B2
Fuzeta P	30	C1

G

Gabarret F	8	B2
Gaillac F	9	F1
Galdar E	43	c1
Galizano E	6	A2
Gallargues F	19	E3
Gallur E	15	E1
Gan F	16	B3
Gandesa E	27	E2
Gandia E	36	C1
Ganges F	19	D3
Garraf E	28	B2
Garray E	14	C1
Garrovillas E	22	B2
Garrucha E	41	F2
Gasteiz/Vitoria E	14	C3
Gaucín E	39	D2
Gavarnie F	16	C2
Gavião P	21	E2
Gelida E	28	B2
Génolhac F	19	E4
Gérgal E	41	D2
Gernika/Lumo E	6	C2
Gerona/Girona E	29	D3
Getafe E	24	B2
Getxo/Algorta E	6	B2
Gibraleón E	31	E1
Gibraltar GBZ	39	D1
Gignac F	19	D3
Gijón E	4	C3
Gimont F	17	E4
Girona/Gerona E	29	D3
Gironella E	28	C3
Góis P	21	E4
Golada E	2	C2
Golegã P	21	D3
Golpejas E	12	B1

50

Gómara E................. 25 F4
Gondrin F................. 8 C2
Gourdon F................ 9 E3
Grado E................... 4 B3
Gramat F.................. 9 F3
Gran Tarajal E........... 43 dl
Granada E................ 40 B2
Granadilla de Abona E.... 43 bl
Grandas de Salime E...... 3 F3
Grândola P............... 30 C4
Granja P................. 10 B2
Graulhet F............... 18 A4
Graus E.................. 16 Cl
Grazalema E.............. 39 D2
Gredos E................. 23 E3
Grenade F................ 8 B2
Grenade F................ 9 El
Grignols F............... 8 C3
Griñón E................. 24 B2
Grisolles F.............. 9 El
Gruissan F............... 18 C2
Guadahortuna E........... 40 C3
Guadalajara E............ 24 C2
Guadalcanal E............ 32 B2
Guadalmina E............. 39 D2
Guadalupe E.............. 23 Dl
Guadarrama E............. 24 B3
Guadix E................. 40 C2
Guarda P................. 22 A4
Guardamar del Segura E... 42 C3
Guardo E................. 5 D2
Guareña E................ 32 B4
Guarromán E.............. 34 Al
Guetaria E............... 7 D2
Guethary F............... 7 E2
Guijuelo E............... 23 D3
Guimarães P.............. 10 C3
Guincho P................ 20 A2
Guisamo E................ 2 C3
Guitiriz E............... 3 D3
Guîtres F................ 8 C4
Gujan-Mestras F.......... 8 A4
Gumiel de Hizán E........ 14 A2
Guntín E................. 3 D2

H

Hagetmau F............... 8 A2
Haro E................... 14 C3
Hasparren F.............. 7 El
Hellín E................. 35 El
Hendaye F................ 7 D2
Herencia E............... 34 C3
Herrera de Pisuerga E.... 13 F4
Herrera del Duque E...... 33 E4
Herreruela E............. 22 A2
Híjar E.................. 26 C2
Hinojosa del Duque E..... 33 D2
Homps F.................. 18 B2
Hondarribia/Fuenterrabía E 7 D2
Honrubia E............... 35 E3
Hontoria del Pinar E..... 14 Bl
Horcajo de Santiago E.... 34 C4
Hornos E................. 41 E4
Hortezuela E............. 25 D4
Hortigüela E............. 14 B2
Hossegor F............... 7 E2
Hostalrich E............. 29 D3
Hostens F................ 8 B3
Houeillès F.............. 8 C3

Hoyos E.................. 22 B3
Huelma E................. 40 C3
Huelva E................. 31 El
Huércal-Overa E.......... 41 F2
Huesca E................. 16 Bl
Huéscar E................ 41 E3
Huete E.................. 25 Dl

I

Ibeas de Juarros E....... 14 B3
Ibi E.................... 43 D4
Iciar E.................. 6 Cl
Igualada E............... 28 B3
Illano E................. 3 F3
Illar E.................. 41 D2
Illescas E............... 24 B2
Inca E................... 45 D3
Infiesto E............... 5 D3
Irun E................... 7 Dl
Iruñea/Pamplona E........ 15 E3
Irurita E................ 15 E4
Irurzun E................ 15 E3
Isaba E.................. 16 A3
Iscar E.................. 13 Dl
Isla E................... 6 A2
Isla Cristina E.......... 31 Dl
Isona E.................. 28 A4
Istres F................. 19 F2
Itxassou F............... 7 El
Izeda P.................. 11 F3
Iznájar E................ 40 A3
Iznalloz E............... 40 C3

J

Jaca E................... 16 B2
Jadraque E............... 25 D3
Jaén E................... 40 B4
Jandia Playa E........... 43 dl
Jaraicejo E.............. 22 C2
Jaraiz E................. 23 D2
Jarandilla E............. 23 D3
Jávea/Xàbia E............ 43 E4
Jerez de la Frontera E... 38 B3
Jerez de los Caballeros E 31 F3
Jijona E................. 43 D4
Jimena E................. 40 C4
Jimena de la Frontera E.. 39 D2
Jódar E.................. 40 C4
Joyeuse F................ 19 E4
Juillac F................ 9 E4
Jumilla E................ 42 B4
Junqueira P.............. 11 E2

L

L'Albi E................. 27 F3
L'Alcúdia E.............. 36 B2
L'Alcúdia de Crespins E.. 36 Bl
L'Aldea E................ 27 El
L'Ametlla de Mar E....... 27 El

L'Ampolla E.............. 27 El
L'Escala E............... 29 E3
L'Espluga de Francoli E.. 27 F2
L'Estartit E............. 29 E3
L'Hospitalet de l'Infant E 27 F2
L'Isle-de-Noé F.......... 17 D4
L'Isle-en-Dodon F........ 17 D3
L'Isle-Jourdain F........ 17 E4
La Alamedilla E.......... 23 F3
La Alberca E............. 22 C3
La Albuera E............. 32 A4
La Almarcha E............ 35 E4
La Almolda E............. 27 D3
La Almunia de Doña Godina E 26 B3
La Antilla E............. 31 El
La Bañeza E.............. 12 C4
La Barrela E............. 3 D2
La Barrosa E............. 38 B2
La Bastide de-Sérou F.... 17 E2
La Bisbal E.............. 29 E3
La Bóveda de Toro E...... 12 Cl
La Calzada de Calatrava E 34 A2
La Carlota E............. 39 E4
La Carolina E............ 34 Al
La Cava E................ 27 El
La Cavalerie F........... 18 C4
La Coruña/A Coruña E..... 2 C4
La Espina E.............. 4 B3
La Gineta E.............. 35 E2
La Granadella E.......... 27 E2
La Grand-Combe F......... 19 E4
La Grande-Motte F........ 19 E3
La Granja E.............. 24 B3
La Guardia E............. 24 Bl
La Hermida E............. 5 E2
La Iglesuela del Cid E... 26 Cl
La Isla E................ 5 D3
La Jonquera E............ 29 E4
La Laguna E.............. 43 bl
La Línea de la Concepción E 39 Dl
La Luisiana E............ 39 E4
La Magdalena E........... 4 B2
La Malène F.............. 19 D4
La Manga del Mar Menor E. 42 C2
La Molina E.............. 28 C4
La Mongie F.............. 16 C2
La Mudarra E............. 13 D2
La Muela E............... 26 B4
La Nava de Ricomalillo E. 23 El
La Oliva E............... 43 d2
La Paca E................ 41 F3
La Palma del Condado E... 31 Fl
La Platja d'Aro E........ 29 E3
La Pobla de Segur E...... 17 Dl
La Pola de Gordón E...... 4 C2
La Puebla de Cazalla E... 39 D3
La Puebla de Montalbán E. 23 Fl
La Puebla de Valverde E.. 36 B4
La Rambla E.............. 39 F4
La Réole F............... 8 C3
La Robla E............... 4 C2
La Roca de la Sierra E... 22 Al
La Roca del Vallés E..... 28 C2
La Roda E................ 35 E3
La Roque-Gageac F........ 9 E3
La Salvetat F............ 9 F2
La Salvetat-sur-Agout F.. 18 B3
La Seu d'Urgell E........ 17 El
La Solana E.............. 34 B2
La Vecilla E............. 4 C2
Labastide-d'Armagnac F... 8 B2
Labastide-Murat F........ 9 E3
Labenne F................ 7 E2
Labouheyre F............. 8 A3

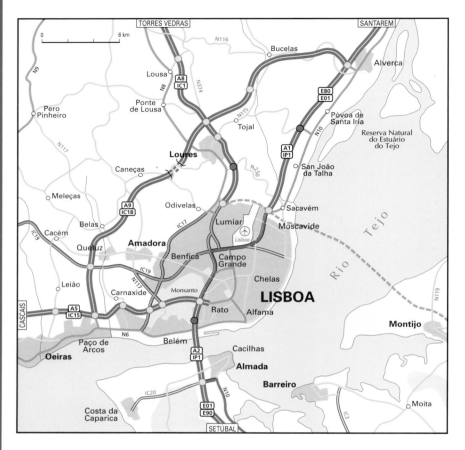

Labrède *F*	8	B4
Labrit *F*	8	B3
Lacalahorra *E*	40	C2
Lacapelle-Marival *F*	9	F3
Lacaune *F*	18	C3
Lacq *F*	16	B4
Ladoeiro *P*	21	F3
Lafrançaise *F*	9	E2
Lagoa *P*	30	B1
Lagos *P*	30	B1
Lagrasse *F*	18	B2
Laguardia *E*	14	C3
Laguépie *F*	9	F2
Lalín *E*	2	C2
Lalinde *F*	9	D4
Lamalou-les-Bains *F*	18	C3
Lamego *P*	11	D2
Landete *E*	36	A4
Langoiran *F*	8	B4
Langon *F*	8	B3
Lanjarón *E*	40	B2
Lannemezan *F*	16	C3
Laplume *F*	8	C2
Larche *F*	9	E4
Laredo *E*	6	B2
Laroque-des-Arcs *F*	9	E3
Larrau *F*	16	A3
Laruns *F*	16	B3
Las Cabezas de San Juan *E*	38	C3
Las Caldas de Besaya *E*	5	F2
Las Campanas *E*	15	E3
Las Navas del Marqués *E*	24	A3
Las Negras *E*	41	E1
Las Palmas de Gran Canaria *E*	43	c1
Las Pedroñeras *E*	35	D3
Las Rozas *E*	24	B2
Las Ventas con Peña Aguilera *E*	23	F1
Laujar de Andarax *E*	41	D2
Lautrec *F*	18	B3
Lauzerte *F*	9	D2
Lauzun *F*	9	D3
Lavardac *F*	8	C2
Lavaur *F*	18	A4
Lavelanet *F*	17	F2
Lavre *P*	20	C1
Laxe *E*	2	B4
Le Barp *F*	8	A4
Le Boulou *F*	18	B1
Le Bugue *F*	9	D4
Le Cap-d'Agde *F*	19	D2
Le Caylar *F*	19	D3
Le Fossat *F*	17	E3
Le Grau-du-Roi *F*	19	E3
Le Mas-d'Azil *F*	17	E2
Le Muret *F*	8	A3
Le Perthus *F*	29	D4
Le Rozier *F*	19	D4
Le Teil *F*	19	F4
Le Vigan *F*	19	D4
Lebrija *E*	38	C3
Lécera *E*	26	C3
Lectoure *F*	8	C2
Ledesma *E*	12	B1
Lédignan *F*	19	E3
Ledigos *E*	13	E3
Léguevin *F*	17	E3
Legutiano *E*	14	C4
Leiria *P*	20	C3
Lekeitio *E*	6	C2
Lekunberri *E*	15	E3
Lembeye *F*	16	C4
León *E*	4	C2
Léon *F*	7	E2
Lepe *E*	31	E1
Lérida/Lleida *E*	27	E3
Lerma *E*	14	A2
Lés *E*	17	D2
Les Baux-de-Provence *F*	19	F3
Les Borges Blanques *E*	27	E3
Les Cabannes *F*	17	F2
Les Escaldes *AND*	17	E1
Les Eyzies-de-Tayac *F*	9	E4
Les Vans *F*	19	E4
Lesjaverk *N*	153	F4

Lestelle Bétharram F	16	B3	Lodosa E	15	D2	Luarca E	4	B4
Leucate F	18	C2	Loeches E	24	C2	Lubia E	14	C1
Leyre E	15	F2	Logroño E	14	C2	Lucena E	39	F3
Lézignan-Corbières F	18	B2	Logrosán E	23	D1	Lucena del Cid E	36	C4
Libourne F	8	C4	Loja E	40	A3	Luciana E	33	F3
Lillo E	34	C4	Lombez F	17	E3	Lugo E	3	D2
Limogne-en-Quercy F	9	F2	Lopera E	33	E1	Lugones E	4	C3
Limoux F	18	A2	Lora del Rio E	32	C1	Lumbier E	15	F2
Linares E	34	A1	Lorca E	42	A3	Lumbrales E	11	F1
Linares de Riofrío E	23	D4	Lormont F	8	B4	Lumo/Gernika E	6	C2
Lindoso P	11	D4	Los Alcázares E	42	C2	Lunas E	18	C3
Liria E	36	B3	Los Arcos E	15	D3	Lunel F	19	E3
Lisboa P	20	B2	Los Arenales del Sol E	43	D3	Luso P	10	B1
Lisle F	9	E1	Los Barrios E	38	C1	Lussan F	19	F4
Lit-et-Mixe F	7	F3	Los Cristianos E	43	b1	Luz-St-Sauveur F	16	C2
Livernon F	9	F3	Los Llanos de Aridane E	42	a2			
Llafranc E	29	E3	Los Navalmorales E	23	E1			
Llagostera E	29	D3	Los Palacios y Villafranca E	38	C3			
Llançà E	29	E4	Los Urrutias E	42	C2			
Llanes E	5	E3	Losar de la Vera E	23	D3			
Llavorsi E	17	E1	Loulé P	30	C1			
Lleida/Lérida E	27	E3	Lourdes F	16	C3			
Llerena E	32	B2	Louredo P	11	D3	Maçanet de la Selva E	29	D3
Lles E	17	E1	Lourinha P	20	B3	Mação P	21	E3
Llodio E	6	B2	Lousã P	21	D4	Macedo de Cavaleiros P	11	F3
Lloret de Mar E	29	D3	Lousada P	10	C3	Machico P	45	b1
Llucmajor E	45	D3	Lovios E	11	D4	Madrid E	24	B2
Lodève F	19	D3	Luanco E	4	C4	Madridejos E	34	B4

M

53

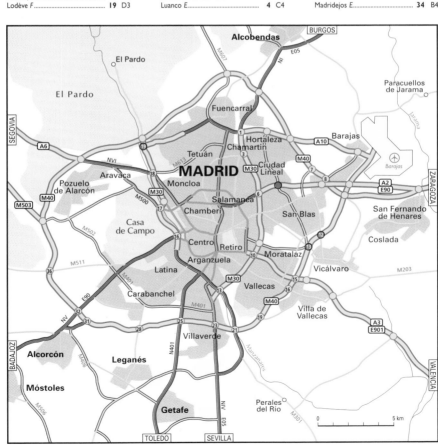

Madrigal de las Altas Torres E	23	F4
Maella E	27	D2
Mafra P	20	B2
Magallón E	15	E1
Magaluf E	44	C3
Magaz E	13	E2
Magescq F	7	F2
Mahora E	35	E2
Maials E	27	E3
Málaga E	39	F2
Malagón E	34	B3
Malpartida de Cáceres E	22	B2
Malpica E	2	B4
Malveira P	20	B2
Manacor E	45	D3
Mancha Real E	40	C4
Mangualde P	10	C1
Manresa E	28	B3
Mansilla de las Mulas E	4	C1
Manteigas P	21	F4
Manzanares E	34	B3
Manzanares el Real E	24	B3
Maó/Mahón E	45	F3
Maqueda E	23	F2
Maranchón E	25	E3
Marateca P	20	C1
Marbella E	39	E2
Marchena E	39	D4
Marcheprime F	8	A4
Marciac F	16	C4
Marcilla E	15	E2
Marín E	2	B2
Marinha Grande P	20	C3
Marmande F	8	C3
Marseillan F	19	D2
Marseillan-Plage F	19	D2
Martel F	9	F4
Martigues F	19	F2
Martín de Yeltes E	22	C4
Martorell E	28	B2
Martos E	40	B4
Marvão P	21	F2
Masegoso de Tajuña E	25	D3
Maspalomas E	43	c1
Massat F	17	E2
Masseube F	17	D3
Matabuena E	24	C4
Matalascañas E	38	B3
Matalebreras E	15	D1
Matallana E	13	D3
Mataró E	28	C2
Matos de Carrico P	20	C4
Matosinhos P	10	B3
Maubourguet F	16	C4
Mauléon-Licharre F	16	A3
Maury F	18	B1
Mauvezin F	9	D1
Mayorga E	13	D3
Mazagón E	38	B4
Mazamet F	18	B3
Mazarrón E	42	B2
Mazères F	17	F3
Mazo E	42	a2
Mealhada P	10	B1
Medellín E	32	C4
Medina de Rioseco E	13	D2
Medina del Campo E	13	D1
Medina-Sidonia E	38	C2
Medinaceli E	25	E3
Meira E	3	E3
Melgaço P	2	B1
Melide E	3	D2
Melides P	30	B4
Mendavia E	15	D2
Mengibar E	40	B4
Mequinenza E	27	E3
Mera E	3	D4
Mérida E	32	B4
Mértola P	31	D2
Mesão Frio P	11	D2
Mesón do Vento E	2	C3
Meyrueis F	19	D4
Mèze F	19	D2
Mézin F	8	C2
Miajadas E	32	C4
Miami Platja E	27	F2
Miélan F	17	D3
Mieres E	4	C3
Mijas E	39	E2
Millas F	18	B1
Millau F	18	C4
Mimizan F	7	F3
Mimizan-Plage F	7	F3
Minglanilla E	35	F3
Mira E	36	A3
Mira P	10	B1
Miraflores de la Sierra E	24	B3
Miramar P	10	B3
Miramas F	19	F2
Miramont-de-Guyenne F	8	C3
Miranda de Ebro E	14	C3
Miranda do Douro P	12	A2
Mirande F	17	D4
Mirandela P	11	E3
Mirantes E	4	B2
Miravalles E	6	B2
Miravet E	27	E2
Mirepoix F	17	F2
Mitrena P	20	B1
Moaña E	2	B2
Mogadouro P	11	F2
Mogón E	41	D4
Moguer E	31	E1
Moiá E	28	C3
Moimenta da Beira P	11	D2
Moissac F	9	D2
Moita P	20	B1
Mojácar E	41	F2
Moledo P	10	C4
Molières F	9	E2
Molina de Aragón E	25	F2
Molins de Rei E	28	C2
Mollet E	28	C2
Mombeltrán E	23	E3
Monachil E	40	B2
Monção P	2	B1
Monchique P	30	B2
Moncófar E	36	C3
Mondariz Balneario E	2	B1
Mondim de Basto P	11	D3
Mondoñedo E	3	E3
Mondragón E	15	D4
Monesterio E	32	B2
Monflanquin F	9	D3
Monforte P	21	E1
Monforte de Lemos E	3	D1
Monóvar E	42	C4
Monpazier F	9	D3
Monreal E	15	E3
Monreal del Campo E	26	A2
Monroyo E	27	D2
Monségur F	8	C3
Mont-de-Marsan F	8	B2
Mont-Louis F	18	A1
Montagnac F	19	D3
Montaigu-de-Quercy F	9	D3
Montalbán E	26	B2
Montamarta E	12	B2
Montañana E	26	C4
Montánchez E	22	B1
Montaren F	19	E4
Montargil P	21	D2
Montastruc la-Conseillère F	17	F4
Montauban F	9	E2
Montbazens F	9	F2
Montblanc E	28	A2
Montcuq F	9	E2
Monte Clérigo P	30	B2
Monte Gordo P	31	D1
Montealagre del Castillo E	35	F1
Montefrío E	40	B3
Montehermoso E	22	C3
Montélimar F	19	F4
Montemor-o-Novo P	20	C1
Monterroso E	3	D2
Montesquieu-Volvestre F	17	E3
Montesquiou F	17	D4
Montfort F	7	F2
Montgat E	28	C2
Montgiscard F	17	F3
Montignac F	9	E4
Montijo P	20	B1
Montijo E	32	B4
Montilla E	39	F4
Montorio E	14	A3
Montoro E	33	E1
Montpellier F	19	D3
Montpezat F	9	E2
Montpon-Ménestérol F	8	C4
Montréal F	8	C2
Montréal F	18	A2
Montréjeau F	17	D3
Montseny E	28	C3
Monzón E	27	E4
Mora P	21	D1
Mora E	34	B4
Móra d'Ebre E	27	E2
Mora de Rubielos E	36	C4
Móra la Nova E	27	E2
Moraira E	43	E4
Morasverdes E	22	C4
Moratalla E	42	A4
Morcenx F	8	A3
Moreda E	40	C3
Morella E	27	D1
Morlaàs F	16	B3
Morón de Almazán E	25	E4
Morón de la Frontera E	39	D3
Móstoles E	24	B2
Mota del Cuervo E	35	D3
Mota del Marques E	13	D2
Motilla del Palancar E	35	E3
Motril E	40	B2
Moura P	31	E3
Mourão P	31	E3
Mouthoumet F	18	B2
Muelas del Pan E	12	B2
Mugron F	8	A2
Mula E	42	B3
Munera E	35	D2
Mungia E	6	C2
Muñico E	23	E3
Muniesa E	26	C2
Muranzel P	10	B2
Murat-sur-Vèbre F	18	C3
Murça P	11	E3
Murcia E	42	B3
Muret F	17	E3
Murguia E	14	C4
Muros E	2	B3
Murtosa P	10	B2
Muskiz E	6	B2

54

Mussidan F 9 D4
Mutrico E 6 C2

N

Nadela E 3 D2
Nailloux F 17 F3
Najac F 9 F2
Nájera E 14 C3
Nalzen F 17 F2
Nanclares de Oca E 14 C3
Nant F 19 D4
Narbonne E 18 C2
Narbonne-Plage F 18 C2
Nava E 4 C3
Nava de la Asunción E 24 A4
Nava del Rey E 12 C1
Navahermosa E 23 F1
Navalcarnero E 24 B2
Navalmanzano E 24 B4
Navalmoral de la Mata E 23 D2
Navalperal E 24 A3
Navarrenx F 16 B4
Navarrete E 14 C2
Navas de San Juan E 34 B1
Navas del Rey E 24 A2
Navatalgordo E 23 F3
Navia E 4 A4
Nazare P 20 C3
Neauvic F 9 D4
Neda E 3 D4
Nelas P 10 C1
Nérac F 8 C2
Nerja E 40 B2
Niebla E 31 F1
Nijar E 41 E1
Nîmes F 19 E3
Nisa P 21 E2
Noain E 15 E3
Nogaro F 8 B2
Noia E 2 B3
Noja E 6 A2
Novelda E 42 C4
Noves F 19 F3
Nuévalos E 26 A3
Nules E 36 C3

O

O Barco de Valdeorras E 3 E1
O Cádabo/Baleira E 3 E2
O Grove E 2 B2
Óbidos P 20 B3
Ocaña E 24 B1
Ochagavia E 15 F3
Odeceixe P 30 B2
Odeleite P 31 D1
Odemira P 30 B2
Ofir P 10 B3
Oia/Arrabal E 2 A1
Ojén E 39 E2
Olargues F 18 C3
Olazagutía E 15 D3
Oleiros E 2 B2
Oleiros E 21 E3
Olette F 18 A1

Olhão P 30 C1
Olite E 15 E2
Oliva E 36 C1
Olivares de Júcar E 35 E4
Oliveira de Azeméis P 10 B2
Oliveira de Frades P 10 C2
Oliveira do Bairro P 10 B1
Oliveira do Hospital P 21 E4
Olivenza E 31 F4
Olmedillo de Roa E 13 F2
Olmedo E 13 D1
Olmillos de Sasamón E 13 F3
Olonzac F 18 B2
Oloron-Ste-Marie F 16 B3
Olot E 29 D4
Olvega E 15 D1
Olvera E 39 D3
Oña E 14 B3
Onda E 36 C3
Ondara E 36 C1
Ontinyent E 36 B1
Ontur E 35 F1
Orange F 19 F4
Orcera E 34 C1
Ordes E 2 C3
Ordino AND 17 E1
Orduña E 6 B1
Orense/Ourense E 2 C1
Orgaz E 34 B4
Orihuela E 42 C3
Orihuela del Tremedal E 25 F2
Orio E 7 D1
Órjiva E 40 C2
Orol E 3 E4
Oropesa E 23 E2
Oropesa del Mar E 37 D3
Orthez F 7 F1
Ortigueira E 3 D4
Oseja de Sajambre E 5 D2
Osera E 26 C3
Osorno E 13 E3
Ossa de Montiel E 34 C2
Ostiz E 15 E3
Osuna E 39 E3

Otero de Bodas E 12 B3
Ourense/Orense E 2 C1
Ourique P 30 C2
Oust F 17 E2
Ovar P 10 B2
Oviedo E 4 C3

P

Padron E 2 B2
Padul E 40 B2
Palacios de Sanabria E 12 A3
Palacios del Sil E 4 A2
Palafrugell E 29 E3
Palamós E 29 E3
Palas de Rei E 3 D2
Palavas-les-Flots F 19 E3
Palencia E 13 E2
Palheiros de Mira P 10 B1
Palheiros de Quiaios P 10 A1
Palheiros de Tocha P 10 A1
Palma E 44 C3
Palma del Rio E 32 C1
Palma Nova E 44 C3
Palmela P 20 B1
Palomares E 41 F2
Pamiers F 17 F2
Pampilhosa da Serra P 21 E3
Pamplona/Iruñea E 15 E3
Panassac F 17 D3
Pancorvo E 14 B3
Panes E 5 E3
Panxon E 2 B1
Paredes P 10 C3
Paredes de Nava E 13 E3
Parentis-en-Born F 7 F3
Pas de la Casa AND 17 F1
Pasaia E 7 D1
Pastrana E 25 D2
Pau F 16 B3

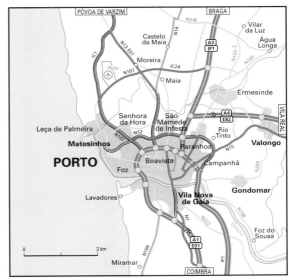

56

Pavia P	21	D1
Payrac F	9	E3
Peal de Becerro E	41	D4
Pedras Salgadas P	11	D3
Pedraza E	24	C4
Pedro Muñoz E	34	C3
Pego E	36	C1
Peguera E	44	C3
Peidralaves E	23	F2
Pellegrue F	8	C4
Penacova P	21	E4
Penafiel P	10	C3
Penafiel E	13	E1
Penamacor P	22	A3
Penaranda E	14	A1
Peñaranda de Bracamonte E	23	E4
Peñarroya-Pueblonuevo E	33	D2
Penas de S Pedro E	35	E1
Penela P	21	D4
Peniche P	20	B3
Peñíscola E	37	E4
Peralejos de las Truchas E	25	F2
Perales del Alfambra E	26	B2
Peralta E	15	E2
Pereiro P	31	D2
Périgueux F	9	D4
Perpignan F	18	B1
Petrá E	45	D3
Peyrehorade F	7	F2
Pézenas F	19	D3
Pias P	31	E3
Picacho de Veleta E	40	C2
Piedrabuena E	33	F3
Piedrafita de Babia E	4	B3
Piedrahita E	23	E3
Pierrefitte-Nestalas F	16	C3
Pierrelatte F	19	F4
Pierroton F	8	B4
Pilat-Plage F	7	F4
Pina de Ebro E	26	C3
Pineda de Mar E	29	D2
Pinhel P	11	E1
Pinos Puente E	40	B3
Pinoso E	42	C4
Pissos F	8	A3
Plaisance F	8	B1
Plasencia E	22	C3
Playa Blanca E	43	d2
Playa de las Americas E	43	b1
Playa de San Juán E	43	D4
Plentzia E	6	B2
Pobes E	14	C3
Podensac F	8	B4
Pola de Allande E	4	A3
Pola de Laviana E	4	C3
Pola de Lena E	4	C3
Pola de Siero E	4	C3
Pola de Somiedo E	4	B3
Pola de Trives E	3	D1
Pollença E	45	D4
Pombal P	21	D4
Ponferrada E	3	F1
Pont-de-Salars F	18	C4
Pont-St-Esprit F	19	F4
Ponta do Sol P	45	a1
Pontacq F	16	C3
Pontão P	21	D3
Ponte Barxas E	2	C1
Ponte Caldelas E	2	B2
Ponte da Barca P	10	C4
Ponte de Lima P	10	C4
Ponte de Sor P	21	D2
Ponteareas E	2	B1
Pontecesures/Enfesta E	2	B2
Pontedeume E	3	D4
Pontevedra E	2	B2
Ponts E	28	A3
Porcuna E	40	B4
Porriño E	2	B1
Port-Barcarès F	18	C1
Port-Camargue F	19	E2
Port d'Alcúdia E	45	D4
Port d'Andratx E	44	C3
Port de Pollença E	45	D4
Port de Sóller E	45	D4
Port-de-Bouc F	19	F2
Port-Leucate F	18	C1
Port-la-Nouvelle F	18	C2
Port-St-Louis-du-Rhône F	19	F2
Port-Ste-Marie F	8	C3
Port-Vendres F	29	E4
Portalegre P	21	E2
Portalrubio E	26	B2
Portbou E	29	E4
Portel P	31	D3
Portela de Messines P	30	C1
Portela do Homem E	11	D4
Portelo P	12	A3
Portimão P	30	B1
Portinatx E	44	B3
Porto P	10	B3
Porto Cristo E	45	D3
Porto da Cruz P	45	b2
Porto de Mós P	20	C3
Porto do Son E	2	B3
Porto Moniz P	45	a2
Portomarin E	3	D2
Portomouro E	2	C3
Porzuna E	34	A3
Posadas E	33	D1
Potes E	5	E2
Pouyastruc F	16	C3
Póvoa de Lanhoso P	10	C3
Póvoa de Varzim P	10	B3
Pozo Alcón E	41	D3
Pozoblanco E	33	D2
Pozuelo de Ariza E	25	F4
Pozuelo de Zarzón E	22	C3
Prades F	18	A1
Pradillo E	14	C2
Praia da Rocha P	30	B1
Praia de Santa Cruz P	20	B2
Praia Grande P	20	A2
Prats de Llucanés E	28	C3
Prats-de-Mollo-la-Preste F	29	D4
Pravia E	4	B4
Premiá de Mar E	28	C2
Priego E	25	E2
Priego de Córdoba E	40	A3
Proença-a-Nova P	21	E3
Puçol E	36	C3
Puebla de Alcocer E	33	D3
Puebla de Don Fadrique E	41	E4
Puebla de Don Rodrigo E	33	E3
Puebla de Lillo E	4	C2
Puebla de Obando E	22	A1
Puebla de Sanabria E	12	A3
Puebla Tornesa E	37	D4
Puente la Reina E	15	E3
Puente Viesgo E	5	F2
Puente-Genil E	39	F3
Puentelarra E	14	C3
Puerto Banús E	39	E2
Puerto Castilla E	23	D3
Puerto de la Cruz E	43	b1
Puerto de Mazarrón E	42	B2
Puerto de San Vicente E	23	D1
Puerto del Carmen E	43	d2
Puerto del Rosario E	43	d1
Puerto Lápice E	34	B3
Puerto Lastres E	5	D3
Puerto Real E	38	B2
Puerto Rico E	43	c1
Puerto-Lumbreras E	41	F2
Puertollano E	33	F2
Puigcerda E	17	F1
Puivert E	18	A2
Punta Umbria E	38	A4
Puntagorda E	42	a2
Purchena E	41	E2
Puy-l'Evêque F	9	E3
Puylaurens F	18	A3
Pyla-sur-Mer F	7	F4

Q

Quarteira P	30	C1
Quesada E	41	D4
Quillan E	18	A2
Quintana de la Serena E	32	C3
Quintana del Puente E	13	E2
Quintanaortuño E	14	A3
Quintanar de la Orden E	34	C4
Quintanar de la Sierra E	14	B2
Quintanilha P	12	A3
Quinto E	26	C3
Quiroga E	3	D1
Quissac F	19	E3

R

Rábade E	3	D3
Rabastens F	9	E1
Rabastens-de-Bigorre F	16	C3
Ramacastañas E	23	E2
Ramales de la Victoria E	6	A2
Rascafria E	24	B3
Réalmont F	18	B4
Rebordelo P	11	E3
Redondela E	2	B2
Redondo P	31	E4
Regua P	11	D2
Reguengos de Monsaraz P	31	E3
Reinosa E	5	E2
Remoulins F	19	F3
Renteria E	7	D1
Requena E	36	A3
Réquista F	18	B4
Retama E	33	F3
Reus E	27	F2
Revel F	18	A3
Riaño E	5	D2
Riaza E	24	C4
Riba de Aire P	10	C3
Ribadavia E	2	C1
Ribadelago E	12	A4
Ribadeo E	3	F3
Ribadesella E	5	D3
Ribeira Brava P	45	a1
Ribera/Santa Eugenia E	2	B2
Ribes de Freser E	28	C4
Ricla E	26	B4
Rieumes F	17	E3
Rieupeyroux F	9	F2

Rieux F 17 E3
Rincón de la Victoria E 39 F2
Rio Maior P 20 C3
Riomar E .... 27 EI
Riopar E .... 35 DI
Riotinto E 31 F2
Ripoll E 28 C4
Riscle E 8 B2
Rivesaltes F .... 18 BI
Roa E .... 13 FI
Robledo de Chavela E 24 A3
Rocamadour F 9 F3
Rodrigatos E 4 B2
Rogil P 30 B2
Roncal E 16 A3
Roncesvalles E 15 F3
Ronda E 39 D2
Roquefort F 8 B2
Roquefort-sur-Soulzon F 18 C4
Roquetas de Mar E .... 41 DI
Rosal de la Frontera E 31 E2
Roses E 29 E4
Rostassac F 9 E3
Rota E 38 B3
Roujan F 18 C3
Rubena E 14 A3
Rubielos de Mora E 36 C4
Ruidera E 34 C2
Rute E 40 A3

S

S Luis P 30 B3
S Marcos de Ataboeira P 31 D2
S'Agaró E 29 E3
S'Algar E 45 F3
S'Arenal E 44 C3
Sa Calobra E 45 D4
Sabadell E 28 C2
Sabiñánigo E 16 B2
Sabres F 8 A3
Sabrosa P 11 D2
Sabugal P 22 A4
Sacedón E 25 D2
Sadaba E 15 E2
Sagres P .... 30 AI
Sagunto E 36 C3
Sahagún E 13 D3
Saillagouse F .... 17 FI
St-Affrique F 18 C4
St-Ambroix F 19 E4
St-André-de-Cubzac F 8 B4
St-Antonin-Noble-Val F 9 E2
St-Béat F 17 D2
St-Beauzély F 18 C4
St-Bertrand-de-Comminges F 17 D3
St-Céré F 9 F3
St-Chamas F 19 F2
St-Chinian F 18 C3
St-Clar F 9 D2
St-Cyprien F 9 E4
St-Cyprien-Plage F .... 18 CI
St-Emilion F 8 C4
St-Étienne-de-Baigorry F 15 F4
St-Gaudens F 17 D3
St-Geours-de-Maremne F 7 E2
St-Gervais F 18 C3
St-Géry F 9 E3
St-Gilles F 19 E3
St-Girons F 17 E2

St-Girons-Plage F 7 E3
St-Hippolyte-du-Fort F 19 E3
St-Jean-de-Luz F 7 E2
St-Jean-du-Bruel F 19 D4
St-Jean-du-Gard F 19 E4
St-Jean-Pied-de-Port F 15 F3
St-Jory F 17 F4
St-Julien F 17 E3
St-Justin F 8 B2
St-Lary-Soulan F 16 C2
St-Lys F 17 E3
St-Macaire F 8 B3
St-Martin-de-Londres F 19 D3
St-Martory F 17 D3
St-Palais F 16 A4
St-Paul-Cap-de-Joux F 18 A3
St-Paul-de-Fenouillet F 18 B2
St-Pé F 16 C3
St-Pierre-de-Chignac F 9 D4
St-Pons F 18 C3
St-Rémy-de-Provence F 19 F3
St-Rome-de-Tarn F 18 C4
St-Sernin-sur-Rance F 18 B4
St-Sever F 8 A2
St-Symphorien F 8 B3
St-Vincent-de-Tyrosse F 7 E2
Ste-Croix-Volvestre F 17 E3
Ste-Enimie F 19 D4
Ste-Foy-la-Grande F 8 C4
Ste-Hélène F 8 A4
Ste-Marie-de-Campan F 16 C3
Stes-Maries-de-la-Mer F 19 E2
Saissac F 18 A3
Salamanca E .... 12 BI
Salardú E 17 D2
Salas E 4 B3
Salas de los Infantes E 14 B2
Saldaña E 13 E4
Salema P .... 30 AI
Salies-de-Béarn F .... 7 FI
Salies-du-Salat F 17 D3
Salignac-Eyvigues F 9 E4
Salinas E 4 C4
Sallent de Gállego E 16 B2

Salles F 8 A4
Salles F 17 F3
Salles-Curan F 18 C4
Salobreña E 40 B2
Salou E 27 F2
Salses-le-Château F .... 18 CI
Salvaterra de Magos P 20 C2
Salvaterra de Miño E .... 2 BI
Salvatierra E 15 D3
Salviac F 9 E3
Sama de Langreo E 4 C3
Samadet F 8 A2
Samatan F 17 E3
Samitier E .... 16 CI
Samos E 3 E2
San Anton Leitza E 15 E4
San Bartolomé de la Torre E ...... 31 EI
San Clemente E 35 D3
San Cosme/Barreiros E 3 E3
San Emiliano E 4 B2
San Esteban de Gormaz E .... 14 BI
San Fernando E 38 B2
San Javier E 42 C3
San José E .... 41 EI
San Juán de Alicante E 43 D4
San Juan del Puerto E .... 31 EI
San Leonardo de Yagüe E .... 14 BI
San Martín de Unx E 15 E2
San Martín de Valdeiglesias E 24 A2
San Martin del Pedroso E 12 A3
San Mateo E .... 27 DI
San Miguel de Bernúy E .... 13 EI
San Miguel de las Dueñas E .... 3 FI
San Millán de la Cogolla E 14 C2
San Nicolás de Tolentino E .... 43 cI
San Pedro de Alcántara E 39 D2
San Pedro del Arroyo E 23 F3
San Pedro del Pinatar E 42 C3
San Pedro do Sul P 10 C2
San Rafael E 24 B3
San Roque E .... 39 DI
San Sebastian de la Gomera E ..... 42 aI
San Sebastián/Donostia E .... 7 DI
San Vincente de la Barquera E 5 E3

57

Sanchidrián E	24	A4
Sancti Spiritus E	22	C4
Sangüesa E	15	F2
Sanguinet F	8	A4
Sanlúcar de Barrameda E	38	B3
Sanlúcar la Mayor E	38	C4
Sant Antoni de Portmany E	44	A3
Sant Carles de la Ràpita E	27	E1
Sant Celoni E	28	C3
Sant Feliu de Guíxols E	29	E3
Sant Françesc de Formentera E	44	A2
Sant Hilari Sacalm E	29	D3
Sant Joan de Labritja E	44	B3
Sant Josep de Sa Talaia E	44	A3
Sant Julià de Lória AND	17	E1
Sant Kurutze Kampezu E	15	D3
Sant Miguel de Balansat E	44	A3
Sant Pere Pescador E	29	E3
Sant Pol de Mar E	29	D2
Sant Quirze de Besora E	28	C3
Sant Sadurni d'Anoia E	28	B2
Santa Bárbara E	31	E2
Santa Clara-a-Velha P	30	B2
Santa Coloma de Farners E	29	D3
Santa Coloma de Queralt E	28	A3
Santa Cristina d'Aro E	29	D3
Santa Cruz P	45	b1
Santa Cruz de la Palma E	42	a2
Santa Cruz de Moya E	36	A4
Santa Cruz de Mudela E	34	B2
Santa Cruz de Tenerife E	43	b1
Santa Elena E	34	B1
Santa Eufemia E	33	D2
Santa Eugenia/Ribera E	2	B2
Santa Eulalia E	26	A2
Santa Galdana E	45	E4
Santa Joan de les Abadesses E	28	C4
Santa María E	45	D3
Santa Maria de Huerta E	25	F3
Santa Marta E	32	A3
Santa Olalla del Cala E	32	B2
Santa Pola E	42	C3
Santa Susana E	29	D2
Sta Comba E	2	B3
Sta Comba Dão P	10	C1
Sta Eulária d'es Riu E	44	B3
Sta María del Campo E	13	F2
Sta María del Páramo E	12	C4
Sta María la Real de Nieva E	24	A4
Santafé E	40	B2
Santana P	45	b2
Santana de Serra P	30	C2
Santander E	6	A2
Santanyi E	45	D3
Santarém P	20	C2
Santed E	26	A3
Santesteban E	15	E4
Santiago de Compostela E	2	C3
Santiago de la Ribera E	42	C3
Santiago do Cacém P	30	B3
Santillana del Mar E	5	F2
Santisteban del Puerto E	34	B1
Santo Tirso P	10	C3
Sto Domingo de la Calzada E	14	C3
Sto Domingo de Silos E	14	A2
Santoña E	6	B2
Santurtzi E	6	B2
Sanxenxo E	2	B2
São Bartolomeu de Messines P	30	C2
São Brás de Alportel P	30	C1
São Domingos P	30	C3
São Gregório P	2	C1
São João da Madeira P	10	B2
São João da Pesqueira P	11	D2
São Marcos da Serra P	30	B2
São Martinho do Porto P	20	B3
São Martinhoe P	21	E4
São Pedro de Muel P	20	C4
São Vicente P	45	a2
Saqués E	16	B2
Saramon F	17	D4
Sariñena E	27	D4
Sarlat-la-Canéda F	9	E4
Sarracin E	14	A3
Sarria E	3	D2
Sarrión E	36	B4
Sarron F	8	B1
Satão P	11	D1
Saucats F	8	B4
Sauve F	19	E3
Sauveterre-de-Béarn F	7	F1
Sauveterre-de-Guyenne F	8	C4
Saverdun F	17	F3
Savignac-les-Eglises F	9	E4
Segorbe E	36	C3
Segovia E	24	B4
Segura E	34	C1
Segura E	22	A3
Segura de León E	32	A2
Segura de los Baños E	26	B2
Seia P	21	F4
Seilhac F	9	F4
Seira E	16	C1
Seixal P	20	B1
Semblana P	30	C2
Sepúlveda E	24	C4
Sequeros E	22	C4
Serém P	10	B2
Serón E	41	E2
Serós E	27	E3
Serpa P	31	D3
Sertã P	21	E3
Sesimbra P	20	B1
Sesma E	15	D2
Sète F	19	D2
Setúbal P	20	B1
Sever P	10	C2
Sévérac-le-Château F	18	C4
Sevilla E	38	C4
Sevilleja de la Jara E	23	E1
Seyches F	8	C3
Sierra Nevada E	40	C2
Sigean F	18	C2
Sigüeiro E	2	C3
Sigüenza E	25	E3
Silla E	36	C2
Silleda E	2	C2
Sils E	29	D3
Silves P	30	B1
Simancas E	13	D2
Sines P	30	B3
Sintra P	20	B2
Siorac-en-Périgord F	9	E4
Sisante E	35	E3
Sitges E	28	B2
Sobrada/Castelo de Paiva P	10	C2
Sobral de Mònte Agraço P	20	B2
Socovos E	41	F4
Solares E	6	A2
Soldeu AND	17	E1
Sóller E	45	D4
Solosancho E	23	E3
Solsona E	28	B4
Sommières F	19	E3
Somosierra E	24	C4
Soncillo E	5	F1
Sonseca E	24	A1
Sopeira E	17	D1
Sorbas E	41	E2
Sore F	8	B3
Soria E	14	C1
Sort E	17	D1
Sos del Rey Católico E	15	F2
Soses E	27	E3
Sotillo de la Adrada E	23	F2
Soto el Real E	24	B3
Sotogrande E	39	D1
Souillac F	9	E4
Soumoulou F	16	C3
Soure P	21	D4
Sousceyrac F	9	F3
Sousel P	21	E1

Soustons *F*	7	E2
Soutelo *E*	2	C2
Suances *E*	5	F3
Sueca *E*	36	C2
Súria *E*	28	B3

T

Tábara *E*	12	B3
Tabernas *E*	41	E2
Tabernes *E*	36	C2
Taboada *E*	3	D2
Tábua *P*	21	E4
Tabuaço *P*	11	D2
Tafalla *E*	15	E2
Talavera de la Reina *E*	23	E2
Talayuelas *E*	36	A4
Tamames *E*	22	C4
Tamarinda *E*	45	E4
Tamarite de Litera *E*	27	E4
Tanger	38	B1
Tapia de Casariego *E*	3	F3
Tarajalejo *E*	43	d1
Tarancón *E*	24	C1
Tarascon *F*	19	F3
Tarascon-sur-Ariège *F*	17	E2
Tarazona *E*	15	D1
Tarazona de la Mancha *E*	35	E3
Tarbes *F*	16	C3
Tardets-Sorholus *F*	16	A3
Tarifa *E*	38	C1
Tarnos *F*	7	E2
Tarragona *E*	28	A2
Tárrega *E*	28	A3
Tartas *F*	8	A2
Tauste *E*	15	E1
Tavira *P*	31	D1
Teguise *E*	43	d2
Telde *E*	43	c1
Telheira *P*	30	B2
Tembleque *E*	34	B4
Tendilla *E*	25	D2
Tenebrón *E*	22	C4
Terradillos de los Templarios *E*	13	D3
Terrassa *E*	28	C2
Terrasson-la-Villedieu *F*	9	E4
Teruel *E*	26	B1
Teulada *E*	43	E4
Thenon *F*	9	E4
Thuir *F*	18	B1
Tinajo *E*	43	d2
Tineo *E*	4	B3
Tirgo *E*	14	C3
Tobarra *E*	35	E1
Tocha *P*	10	A1
Toledo *E*	24	A1
Tomar *P*	21	D3
Tomelloso *E*	34	C3
Tona *E*	28	C3
Tondela *P*	10	C1
Tonneins *F*	8	C3
Tordera *E*	29	D3
Tordesillas *E*	13	D2
Toreno *E*	3	F1
Torija *E*	25	D3
Torla *E*	16	B2
Toro *E*	12	C2
Torrão *P*	30	C4
Torre *E*	40	A2
Torre Baja *E*	36	B4
Torre de la Higuera *E*	38	B4

Torre de Moncorvo *P*	11	E2
Torre del Bierzo *E*	4	A2
Torre del Mar *E*	40	A2
Torre Vã *P*	30	C3
Torreblanca *E*	37	D4
Torredembarra *E*	28	A2
Torredonjimeno *E*	40	B4
Torregamones *E*	12	B2
Torrejón de la Calzada *E*	24	B2
Torrejón el Rubio *E*	22	C2
Torrelaguna *E*	24	C3
Torrelapaja *E*	25	F4
Torrelavega *E*	5	F2
Torrelodonés *E*	24	B3
Torremolinos *E*	39	F2
Torrenostra *E*	37	D4
Torrente de Cinca *E*	27	E3
Torrenueva *E*	40	B1
Torrequemada *E*	22	B1
Torres Novas *P*	21	D3
Torres Vedras *P*	20	B2
Torrevieja *E*	42	C3
Torrijos *E*	24	A2
Torroella de Montgri *E*	29	E3
Tortosa *E*	27	E1
Tossa de Mar *E*	29	D3
Totana *E*	42	A3
Tournay *F*	16	C3
Tournon-d'Agenais *F*	9	D3
Trabadelo *E*	3	E1
Tragacete *E*	25	F1
Trancoso *P*	11	D1
Trebujena *E*	38	C3
Tremp *E*	28	A4
Trie *F*	17	D3
Trindade *P*	11	E2
Tróia *P*	20	B1
Trujillo *E*	22	C1
Tubilla de Agua *E*	14	A4
Tuchan *E*	18	B2
Tudela *E*	15	E1
Tudela de Duero *E*	13	D2
Tui *E*	2	B1
Tuineje *E*	43	d1
Tulle *F*	9	F4
Turégano *E*	24	B4
Turre *E*	41	F2

U

Úbeda *E*	40	C4
Ubrique *E*	39	D2
Ugijar *E*	40	C2
Ulldecona *E*	27	E1
Ulldemolins *E*	27	F2
Unquera *E*	5	E3
Urdos *F*	16	B3
Usagre *E*	32	B3
Ustaritz *F*	7	E1
Utiel *E*	36	A3
Utrera *E*	38	C3
Uzès *F*	19	F3

V

Vagos *P*	10	B2
Valcarlos *E*	15	F3
Valdeltormo *E*	27	D2

Valdemorillo *E*	24	B3
Valdenoceda *E*	14	B4
Valdepeñas *E*	34	B2
Valdoviño *E*	3	D4
Vale de Açor *P*	31	D2
Vale de Cambra *P*	10	C2
Vale do Lobo *P*	30	C1
Valença do Minho *P*	2	B1
Valence *F*	8	C2
Valence *F*	9	D2
Valence d'Albigeois *F*	18	B4
Valencia *E*	36	C2
Valencia de Alcántara *E*	21	F2
Valencia de Don Juan *E*	12	C3
Valencia de las Torres *E*	32	B3
Vall de Uxó *E*	36	C3
Vallado *E*	4	A3
Valladolid *E*	13	D2
Valldemossa *E*	44	C4
Valle de loc Caidos *E*	24	B3
Vallehermoso *E*	42	a1
Valleraugue *F*	19	D4
Vallivana *E*	27	D1
Vallon-Pont-d'Arc *F*	19	F4
Valls *E*	28	A2
Valongo *P*	10	C3
Valpaços *P*	11	E3
Valras-Plage *F*	18	C2
Valtierra *E*	15	E2
Valverde *E*	42	a1
Valverde del Camino *E*	31	F1
Valverde del Fresno *E*	22	B3
Vandellós *E*	27	E2
Varilhes *F*	17	F2
Vauvert *F*	19	E3
Vayrac *F*	9	F4
Vecinos *E*	23	D4
Vegadeo *E*	3	F3
Vejer de la Frontera *E*	38	B2
Vélez Blanco *E*	41	F3
Vélez Rubio *E*	41	F3
Vélez-Málaga *E*	40	A2
Venda de Galizes *P*	21	E4
Venda Nova *P*	11	D3
Vendargues *F*	19	E3
Vendas Novas *P*	20	C1
Venta de Arraco *E*	16	A3
Venta de Cardeña *E*	33	E2
Vera *E*	41	F2
Vera de Bidasoa *E*	7	D1
Verfeil *F*	17	F3
Vergt *F*	9	D4
Verín *E*	11	E4
Vernet *F*	17	E3
Vernet-les-Bains *F*	18	A1
Vézénobres *F*	19	E4
Viana do Alentejo *P*	31	D4
Viana do Bolo *E*	11	F4
Viana do Castelo *P*	10	B4
Vianne *F*	8	C2
Vias *F*	19	D2
Vic *E*	28	C3
Vic-en-Bigorre *F*	16	C3
Vic-Fezensac *F*	8	C2
Vicdessos *F*	17	E2
Vidigueira *P*	31	D3
Viella *E*	17	D2
Vieux-Boucau-les-Bains *F*	7	E2
Vigo *E*	2	B1
Vila de Rei *P*	21	D3
Vila do Bispo *P*	30	A2
Vila do Conde *P*	10	B3
Vila Flor *P*	11	E2
Vila Franca de Xira *P*	20	B2

59

60

Vila Fresca de Azeitão P 20 B1
Vila Nova da Cerveira P 2 B1
Vila Nova de Famalição P 10 C3
Vila Nova de Foz Côa P 11 E2
Vila Nova de Milfontes P 30 B3
Vila Nova de Ourém P 21 D3
Vila Nova de Paiva P 11 D2
Vila Pouca de Aguiar P 11 D3
Vila Praia de Âncora P 10 C4
Vila Real P 11 D3
Vila Real de Santo António P 31 D1
Vila Velha de Ródão P 21 E3
Vila Verde de Ficalho P 31 E2
Vila Viçosa P 31 E4
Vila-rodona E 28 A2
Viladamat E 29 E3
Vilafranca del Penedés E 28 B2
Vilagarcía de Arousa E 2 B2
Vilamoura P 30 C1
Vilanova de Arousa E 2 B2
Vilanova i la Geltrú E 28 B2
Vilar Formoso P 22 B4
Vilassar de Mar E 28 C2
Villa Carlos E 45 F3
Villa Fruela E 13 F2
Villablino E 4 B3
Villacañas E 34 C4
Villacarrillo E 41 D4
Villacastín E 24 A3
Villada E 13 D3
Villadiego E 13 F3
Villafranca de los Barros E 32 B3
Villafranca del Bierzo E 3 E1
Villafranca del Cid E 26 C1
Villafranca Montes de Oca E 14 B3
Villahermosa E 34 C2
Villahoz E 13 F2
Villajoyosa E 43 D4
Villalba E 24 B3
Villalba E 3 D3
Villalba de la Sierra E 25 E1
Villalcázar de Sirga E 13 E3
Villalón de Campos E 13 D3
Villalpando E 12 C3
Villamañán E 12 C4
Villamanin E 4 C2
Villamartin E 39 D3
Villamartín de Campos E 13 E3
Villandraut F 8 B3
Villanueva de Argaño E 13 F3
Villanueva de Córdoba E 33 E2
Villanueva de Gallego E 26 C4
Villanueva de la Serena E 32 C4
Villanueva de la Sierra E 22 C3
Villanueva de la Vera E 23 D2
Villanueva de los Castillejos E 31 E1
Villanueva de los Infantes E 34 C2
Villanueva del Arzobispo E 41 D4
Villanueva del Campo E 12 C3
Villanueva del Fresno E 31 E3
Villanueva del Huerva E 26 B3
Villarcayo E 6 A1
Villardefrades E 12 C2
Villarejo de Salvanés E 24 C2
Villarmayor E 12 B1
Villarreal de los Infantes E 37 D3
Villarreal de S Carlos E 22 C2
Villarrobledo E 35 D3
Villarroya de la Sierra E 26 A4
Villarrubia de los Ojos E 34 B3
Villasrubias E 22 B3
Villastar E 26 B1
Villatobas E 24 C1
Villatoro E 14 A3

Villatoya E 36 A3
Villavelayo E 14 B2
Villaviciosa E 33 D2
Villaviciosa E 4 C3
Villefort F 19 E4
Villefranche-d'Albigeois F 9 F1
Villefranche-de-Lauragais F 17 F3
Villefranche-de-Lonchat F 8 C4
Villefranche-de-Rouergue F 9 F2
Villefranche-du-Périgord F 9 E3
Villemur F 9 E1
Villena E 36 A1
Villeneuve F 9 F2
Villeneuve F 19 F3
Villeneuve-de-Marsan F 8 B2
Villeneuve-sur-Lot F 9 D3
Villeréal F 9 D3
Villoldo E 13 E3
Vimianzo E 2 B3
Vimieiro P 21 D1
Vimioso P 12 A2
Vinaixa E 27 F3
Vinarós E 37 E4
Vinça F 18 B1
Vinhais P 11 F3
Virgen de la Cabeza E 33 F1
Viseu P 10 C1
Viso del Marqués E 34 B2
Vitigudino E 11 F1
Vitoria/Gasteiz E 14 C3
Viveiro E 3 E4
Vivel del Río Martín E 26 B2
Viver E 36 C3
Viviers F 19 F4
Vouzela P 10 C2

X

Xàbia/Jávea E 43 E4
Xàtiva E 36 B1
Xeraco E 36 C1
Xeresa E 36 C1
Xinzo de Limia E 11 E4
Xubia E 3 D4

Y

Yaíza E 43 d2
Yecla E 36 A1
Yesa E 15 F2
Yeste E 35 D1

Z

Zafra E 32 B3
Zahara de los Atunes E 38 C1
Zalamea de la Serena E 32 C3
Zalamea la Real E 31 F2
Zambrana E 14 C3
Zambujeira do Mar P 30 B2
Zamora E 12 B2
Zaragoza E 26 C4

Zarautz E 7 D1
Zorita E 22 C1
Zornotza E 6 C2
Zubiri E 15 E3
Zuera E 26 C4
Zumaia E 6 C2